5-STAR
CUSTOMER SERVICE

In Pursuit of Service & Hospitality Excellence

How to Create and Systematise an
Excellent Customer Service Culture,
Offer Memorable Customer Experiences
and Improve Personal & Organisational
Service Performance Standards.

Archibald T. Marwizi

5-Star Customer Service

All rights reserved. No portion of this book may be reproduced, stored in a retrieval system, or transmitted in any form or by any means – electronic, mechanical, photocopy, recording, scanning or other – except for brief quotations in critical reviews or articles, without the prior written permission of the publisher.

Copyright © 2015
ISBN: 978 - 1 - 5142 - 7328- 9
Archibald T. Marwizi

Published in Harare, Zimbabwe
by Gudbank Investments
t/a Five Star Services

9 Humewood Ave, Southdowns, Gweru, Zimbabwe
Phone: +263-772.292.470
Email: archie@fivestar.co.zw | gudmsd@gmail.com

Websites:
www.fivestar.co.zw

www.archiemarwizi.com

Disclaimer

This book is intended for informational purposes only and does not constitute legal, technical, business strategy or other advice and should not be relied on as such. Each individual and organisation accepts the sole responsibility to interpret and apply information and examples used in this book, in the way suitable for their specific needs. The author does not endorse any product, service, individual or organisation referenced in this book, or its producer or representative. The author and the publisher also does not make any express or implied warranties, or assumes any legal liability for the accuracy, completeness, timeliness or usefulness of any information contained in this book, including links to any websites.

Dedication

To those who care enough to put a Smile on the faces of the ones they serve, because they realise their growth, profitability, sustainability and fulfilment is tied to the level of customer satisfaction they offer.

To those still making an investment to provide quality memorable experiences and building mutually beneficial, profitable relationships...

"A customer is the most important visitor on our premises. He is not dependent on us; we are dependent on him. He is not an interruption on our work; he is the purpose of it. He is not an outsider on our business; he is part of it. We are not doing him a favour by serving him; he is doing a favour by giving us an opportunity to do so."
-Mahatma Gandhi

Thanks

Special thanks to my wife, Sibongile, who has become my writing partner! (She refuses to go to bed without me, so she will sit on the couch, by my side until 3am, occasionally dozing off and serving the much-needed cup of lemon tea – a 5-Star Customer Service Provider and a superb Customer Relationship Manager for the past 17 years indeed!

5-STAR
CUSTOMER SERVICE

In Pursuit of Service & Hospitality Excellence

How to Create and Systematise an
Excellent Customer Service Culture,
Offer Memorable Customer Experiences
and Improve Personal & Organisational
Service Performance Standards.

Archibald T. Marwizi

5-Star Customer Service

CONTENTS

Introduction - No Lack of Opportunity	9
The 5-Star Customer Service Framework	15

STAR 1 – KNOWLEDGE AND SKILLS
Factors Affecting Customer Service	29
Why Service Standards Become Poor	41
Knowledge & Skills Required	53
Back2Basics	75
Understand Your Customers	81
The Ingredients of 5-Star Customer Service	89

STAR 2 – EFFECTIVE COMMUNICATION
Interpersonal Communication	125
Communication Technologies	141

STAR 3 – ATTITUDE & THE PERSONAL BRAND
Intrapersonal Communication	149

STAR 4 – POLICIES, SYSTEMS, PROCESSES & STANDARDS (PSPS)
Policies, Systems, Processes & Standards	161
Steps from Strategy to 5-Star Customer Service	189
Service Charters & Public Institutions	195

STAR 5 – CRM & TEAM DYNAMICS
The 3 Pillars of CRM	215
CRM Systems & Technologies	228
Creating a 5-Star Customer Service Culture	239
Initiatives To Improve Service	244

The 10 Commandments of 5-Star Service	249
Other Books, Author & Reference Index	251

5-Star Customer Service

Introduction

NO LACK OF OPPORTUNITY

"Too many companies see customer experience as a slogan exercise. We realized that if we didn't build our strategy around how customers experience our products, a start-up with that focus could eventually overtake us."
-PHILIP GERSKOVICH

Opportunities will always exist in all markets, including, as I have observed, churches and political parties! The major reason why business opportunities will always exist in every economic sector is because the majority of organizations and businesses are not willing to take customers seriously. Then you have the organizations who don't think they are businesses, therefore they have no customers.

Bad service, negative attitudes and being unresponsive to customer needs and complaints, are all examples of how customers are being taken for granted every day. The lack of excellent service will remain the biggest reason why there will never be a shortage of business opportunities. There is what I call the 'suppliers' market syndrome' – it is an enemy of service excellence. Suppliers who actually believe their customers need them more than they need the customers.

As long as your customers are not happy, you have extended an open invitation for competitors to share or completely take your market over. This applies even to those statutory bodies that enjoy monopolies – either they will be forced to liberalise their sector or they will fuel the "black", "grey" or illegal markets for their services as well as fuel corruption within their institutions, as people seek to access better service provision.

Free tip – wherever you experience bad service becomes your clue and an indication pointing you to a business opportunity in that market! The customers in that market can do with, and will appreciate a better service provider than the existing ones.

I wrote to a very large organisation for input I needed so I could use their organisation as an example and case study in two of my books, including this one. The senior executive responsible for facilitating this process responded timely to my request, as follows:

"Having gone through your book intent, it is my view that your area of focus is especially suited to

the service industries such as hotels and restaurants, airlines, banks, retail stores, telecommunication service providers, etc. Our type of business (mining) is such that we have no marketing personnel, have no direct customers in the real sense, and as such we have no guest/customer feedback systems or loyalty programmes. We do not run any customer service initiatives or programmes. It's really due to the nature of the business that we are in."

Imagine this: The government, impressed by the performance of the organisation managed by the executive mentioned above, decides to appoint him to a senior government position. If the executive was to export and transpose his view and attitude of customers and service (*"no marketing personnel," "no direct customers in the real sense," "no customer feedback systems"* or *"no loyalty programs"*) – What kind of service would you expect from the public service institution or ministry they serve? What kind of culture would they influence?

Another executive from a listed blue-chip company responded, *"The Company does not, of necessity, participate in such projects. Regards."* (Who must participate, if the best do not share their stories? It is such corporate attitudes that limit the growth and improvement of customer service in our different economic sectors.)

Such limited understanding of who customers are, what customer service is all about and the unwillingness to share stories of excellence, will remain what I term in this book, 'the limiters' of 5-Star customer service.

Every organisation and institution, including hospitals, mining houses, the police, government departments, schools, churches and prison services, can and must practice 5-Star Customer Service principles in the context of their line of business and target customers. Beliefs and attitudes must change in line with market expectations. The two examples from the big corporations mentioned above, can be traced and linked to the attitudes they portray through the quality of service and conditions of business to which they expose their suppliers and stakeholders, because they sincerely believe they *"have no direct customers in the real sense."*

If you have people and stakeholders who consume and take up your products and services, if you have employees, co-workers and suppliers – then you can never say you have no customers. You have customers in the most real sense and you need to implement good customer service programmes and initiatives!

Learn to share your story if it will help improve service standards within your organisation, community or economy.

In writing this book and structuring it the way it has been, my objectives included the following:

1. To inspire professionals in all economic sectors by exposing them to what some of the best in Customer Service and Customer Relationship Management are doing.
2. To provide university and professional students with an experience-based Customer Service & CRM reference resource,
3. To avail organisations with an essential corporate library resource; and
4. To provide a comprehensive reference text for our 5-Star Customer Service training workshops, as we train across economic sectors in Africa and beyond.

The tools and principles used in this book to enhance the knowledge-acquisition process, include the following:

1. **Learning Stories**
   A generous dosage of real-life stories have been used as Case Studies to help you learn what to do or what not to do when it comes to providing 5-Star Customer Service.

2. **Learning Questions**
   Each key section and chapter includes important questions that will help you reflect on, and evaluate, your own performance. These questions can be a very useful resource for

group exercises, team briefs and discussions. Use these questions to turn your personal and organisational service performance into 5-Star status.

3. **What the Best In The World Are Doing**
   Throughout the book, you will encounter special sections titled, *"What the Best in the World are doing."* Learn from how some of the best companies and organisation in the world are excelling in providing 5-Star Customer Service. This also includes the study in implementing Citizen Charters to help improve service delivery by government institutions, beginning with initiatives in the UK in 1991. Also includes the inspiring stories of ExtraCity Luxury Coaches, Tony Hsieh and Zappos.com as well as various other examples from some of the Best Global Brands.

4. **Statistics from International Surveys**
   The weight, cost, and business implications of the customer service and relationship management principles covered in the book, are well depicted and supported by numerous statistics from surveys conducted by different respectable sources on the international customer service scene.

Chapter 1

THE 5-STAR CUSTOMER SERVICE FRAMEWORK

Even today, our belief is that our Brand, our Culture, and our Pipeline...are the only competitive advantage that we will have in the long run. Everything else can and will eventually be copied."
- TONY HSIEH | CEO, ZAPPOS.COM

"It felt strange to have gone from the brink of going out of business to such rapid growth over such a short period of time. We didn't know it at the time, but all the hard work and investments we made into customer service and company culture would pave the way for us to hit our goal of $1 billion in gross merchandise sales in 2008 – two years ahead of our original goal of 2010...a big reason we hit our goal early was that we decided to invest our time, money and resources into three key areas: customer service (which would build our brand and drive word of mouth), culture (which would lead to the formation of our core values), and employee training and development (which would eventually lead to the creation of our Pipeline Team). Even today, our belief is that our Brand, our Culture, and our Pipeline...are the only competitive advantage that we will have in the long run. Everything else can and will eventually be copied."
- TONY HSIEH, CEO ZAPPOS.COM

THE 5-STAR CUSTOMER SERVICE FRAMEWORK

If you have gone through the 5 or 7 Ps of Marketing – now it's time you went through the 5 Stars (Pillars) of Customer Service. This will guide you in making Customer Service a key component of your Strategic Plan. This model and approach to Customer Service is meant to translate your daily practices and performance into a sustainable Culture of 5-Star Customer Service (Service Excellence or Excellent Service).

The components of this book are structured on the model depicted in Diagram 1 below.

THE 5-STAR SERVICE EXCELLENCE MODEL

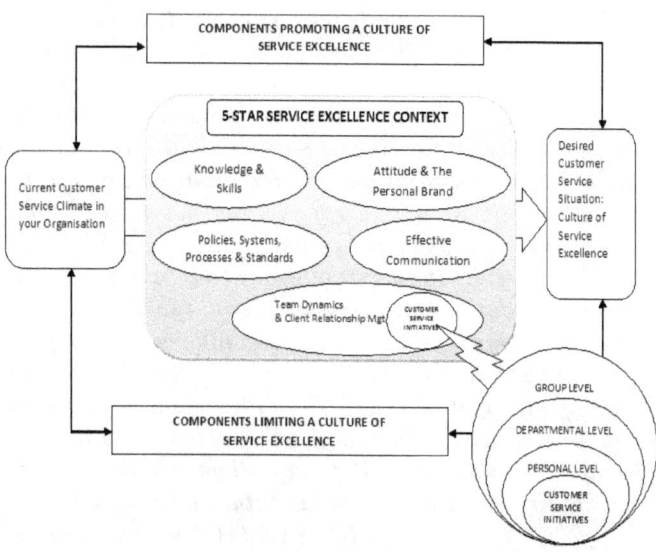

Diagram 1 - 5-Star Customer Service Model[1]

5-Star Customer Service

To provide your customers with 5-Star Customer Service means you must be able to:

1. Make Service Excellence a key part of your Strategy and reflect it through senior management commitment and resource allocation.
2. Enhance the components that promote Service Excellence as a Culture, at individual, departmental and group levels.
3. Reduce or eliminate the components that limit or hinder your chances to practice a Culture of Service Excellence.
4. Have in place policies, systems, processes and standards that enable you to constantly identify and cover the gaps between your prevailing Customer Service quality and your Desired Service Excellence Culture.
5. Use a combination of initiatives and approaches, individually and corporately, in the context of your organisation or work responsibilities, to customize and apply the 5 Pillars of the 5-Star Customer Service Framework, namely:

    a. Knowledge & Skills required to provide excellent (5-Star) customer service.

    b. Effective Communication Skills (Intrapersonal and Interpersonal)

c. Attitude and The Personal Brand – a Personal Responsibility In Delivering Excellence (PRIDE)

d. Policies, Systems, Processes and Standards (PSPS) – Systematising Excellence in Service provision.

e. Customer Relationship Management (CRM) and Team Dynamics.

6. Understand that a 5-Star rating is a Measure and Mark of Excellence, and it takes serious commitment to attain and sustain.

MISCONCEPTIONS ABOUT CUSTOMER SERVICE

First, let's deal with, and dispel, the misconceptions and myths surrounding customer service and customer care. Over the decades as I have travelled around, training and assisting organizations to improve their level of customer satisfaction, I have met some scary views about what workers and people in general think customer service is all about. Most frightening and goose-bump-inducing was the reality that even some senior managers and executives have a wrong view of customer service and its place within the strategy and culture of the organisation.

Some of the views I have encountered include taking customer service as one or more of the following (it is time to get rid of such limited knowledge):

1. **A Sign of weakness**

   There are people who believe that a customer service focus is training people to be *"too nice"*, *"always smiling for nothing"* and then ending up being ineffective. They believe organisation representatives must be tough, firm and even rude, as a sign of confidence and seriousness in what they do.

2. **Security-threat**

   Some believe that customer service training must not be extended to security personnel, including guards, the police and army. They use the points in (1) above to support the reasoning that it becomes a security threat. A head of the security department of a large institution actually refused to release his subordinates to attend a company-wide customer service training on these grounds.

3. **Necessary just for front-office staff and not necessary for managers and back-office or support staff**

   Yet others think that only front line staff dealing with external customers face-to-face, need to have customer service skills. Some even claim that they do not have customers, like the executive I referred to at the beginning of this book.

4. *"Waste of time and money teaching people to smile"*

   Whilst customer service is not just about smiling at customers – I strongly disagree that teaching people to smile would be categorized as a waste of money. Have you ever thought of the Power of a Smile? Learn from the following advertisement placed by one company during the Christmas shopping season.

The Power of a Smile

"It costs nothing, but creates much. It enriches those who receive, without impoverishing those who give. It happens in a flash and the memory of it sometimes lasts forever, None are so rich they can get along without it, and none so poor but are richer for its benefits. It creates happiness in the home, fosters good will in a business, and is the countersign of friends. It is rest to the weary, daylight to the discouraged, sunshine to the sad, and Nature's best antidote for trouble. Yet it cannot be bought, begged, borrowed, or stolen, for it is something that is no earthly good to anybody till it is given away. And if...some of our salespeople should be too tired to give you a smile, may we ask you to leave one of yours? For nobody needs a smile so much as those who have none left to give!"[2]

THE TOOLBOX/RECIPE APPROACH

What people with the above misconceptions fail to appreciate is that customer service provision requires skill. It is also an essential requirement for every individual and organisation that, at any given time, has a visitor, customer or someone depending on them to meet a need, whether in the workplace or the social environment.

A skilled customer service provider grows in the practice of 5-Star Customer Service to the extent of knowing the relevant tool to take out of the 'service tool-box' and relevantly apply to a given situation. They know when to smile and when not to, they know when to seek assistance of the security personnel when dealing with an emotional customer, and when to apply soft-skills to empathise, help the customer to calm down, then find a solution. Great customer service agents know that you cannot change a flat tyre using a spoon and fork – you need the right tools for the job, the right ingredients in the correct quantities for the recipe to come out tasty and memorable – in a pleasant way!

A mining company cannot be expected to adopt the same service standards, policies and initiatives as a hotel, a school, bank or a church organisation. Each must develop the competences and knowledge required to translate the same principles of a 5-Star Customer Service brand into the context of their unique line of business.

Smiling at a disappointed and fuming customer, just because you were taught during training, to use a friendly smile – shows a lack of professional tact in the use of Customer Service tools. Learn to use the Toolbox or Recipe approach - select tools or ingredients relevant for each customer service encounter and you will enjoy providing 5-Star service experiences all the time.

I wish and hope that the current state of your service is lacking in the misconceptions covered above. If you picked any signs resembling some parts of your organisation, then take the time and effort to invest in putting the contents of this book into practice.

Every organisation must think of how to better serve those who depend on them, internally and externally. This means we all need to develop and practice 5-Star Customer Service skills. Your business opportunities are embedded in those customers' needs, and sustaining your business depends on the customers' continued support. This cycle will continue, to the benefit of both parties, as long as you can bring satisfaction and value to your customers.

Take time for introspection and as you go through this book, use the stories and principles covered to identify areas of improvement so you can consciously start to work on improving the level of service you are providing, both personally and as an organisation.

Use the Learning Questions throughout this book to reflect and make necessary changes to the way you serve and treat customers. Benchmark with what the best service providers do and set a challenge for yourself to be counted among the best. Have sectional and departmental discussions, meetings and briefs on specific issues and requirements, for you to continuously improve the experiences of those depending on the output of your work effort.

WHO IS THE CUSTOMER SERVICE PROVIDER OR REPRESENTATIVE?

Whenever we refer to a service provider or customer service representative/agent in this book, we include in the meaning, anyone or any organisation offering a service or products to others, whether internally, externally, in the business world or in the social realm – including at home. It is not just limited to customer service reps/officers, call centre agents, receptionists and sales reps/agents in the so-called *'traditional service industries'* or *'front office'*.

In short – every one of us is a service provider at some point, contrary to the beliefs of the senior executive I mentioned earlier, who felt his organisation did not have customers because they "*do not have marketing personnel* (i.e. they do not sell anything)." This book's view of a customer service provider will be further supported by the definitions of service and hospitality provided in the coming chapters.

EXAMPLES OF BAD SERVICE

Bad customer service leads to loss of customers and increased complaints, both of which can lead to the demise of the organisation or the loss of employment. This book will help you to learn from examples of both, bad customer service and excellent customer service. Besides the stories, statistics from research and surveys conducted in different parts of the world will help paint the picture of the consequences of No (0-Star) service, Bad or Poor (1-2 Star) service, Average (3-Star) service, Good (4-Star) service or Excellent (5-Star) service.

SERVICE-FOCUSED SWOT ANALYSIS

If you look at Diagram 1 again – the evaluation of the difference or gap existing, between your Current Customer Service Climate and your Desired Customer Service Situation (Culture of Service Excellence), is the equivalent of conducting a SWOT Analysis of your organisation or department in respect to Customer Service.

The SWOT Analysis will not be complete without undergoing the process of identifying and addressing the Components Limiting or Promoting a Culture of Service Excellence.

When the above issues are covered, whilst focusing on the internal or micro-customer service environment, you are able to identify your Strengths and Weaknesses as a department or organisation. Focusing on the external/broader or macro-customer service environment opens up your strategic planning process to be able to identify existing Opportunities and Threats to your organisation or industry, based on any market parameters influenced by or influencing different Customer Service dynamics.

To help you kick-start the service-focused SWOT analysis, take time to reflect on the following questions:

LEARNING QUESTIONS

1. What is your current Customer Service Climate and culture? What room for improvement exists?

2. In what ways or roles can you identify yourself as a service provider?

3. What issues threaten the improvement of service offered to customers?

4. What are you already doing well as service providers that you need to build on and keep doing?

5. In your profession or line of business, what are the benefits of attaining a 5-Star Customer Service status?

6. Can you identify any organisation that is excelling in Customer Service? What are they doing to get it right? How is that impacting their overall performance as an organisation?

7. Are you confident of the current quality of knowledge and skills existing in your organisation? Can they deliver the memorable experiences expected of 5-Star Customer Service brands?

Chapter 2

FACTORS AFFECTING EXCELLENT CUSTOMER SERVICE

"62% of global customers switched service providers due to poor customer service experiences."
– ACCENTURE

"A customer is 4 times more likely to buy from a competitor if the problem is service related vs. product or price related."
- BAIN & COMPANY

THE WISHES OF A CUSTOMER TAKEN FOR GRANTED

The wishes of a customer taken for granted are to take their business and custom elsewhere, as soon as they get an alternative.

During a discussion with a friend some time ago, he expressed his wishes, *"The next time I get some money, I am going to sink a borehole, build a septic tank, buy a gas stove, a solar heater and get myself a low-noise generator – then kiss the municipal authority and power utility, goodbye! These people are taking us for granted."*

Never take customers for granted – they will always remember and make you pay, even after decades. The story of what used to be the largest bus company in Zimbabwe, before the transport sector was liberalized, is an awakening reminder. A few other government parastatals and utility providers could be added to the case study on what can happen to an organisation if it takes its customers for granted. Even some once-thriving private business enterprises are now in the *corporate museum* because they took customers for granted. The moment customers get an alternative, they will not even come to bid farewell – the vote with their feet and wallets.

LEARNING STORY

As a student, I used to get ZW$1 as my daily allowance, it was enough for my 18 cents return bus fare, some break and lunch provision and I was disciplined enough to save 20 cents every other day. My only trouble came mostly in the morning, whenever I handed that ZW$1 coin to the bus driver. He would almost always throw it into my face whilst he literally shouted, *"Where do you think I get the change from?"* Whilst I disembarked to look for the coin, the bus would drive off, leaving me to wait for the next one – 30 minutes later. Obviously on such days I would be late for school, with the icing being the punishment through menial assignments.

The buses had a notice sign by the door, it read: *"Pay As You Enter."* This meant a queue going out and along the side of the bus even if it was raining cats and dogs. If there were heavy rains, the bus station shelters would not help. At most times, buses would cruise back to their depot leaving stranded passengers along the way, just because the driver was going to 'knock-off'. It also did not matter how much you motioned for the driver to stop – if you had not yet reached the bus station, you would not get a chance. All this happened for years, even decades – when the winds of change finally came, customers remembered how they were treated before, and they demonstrated how much of 'kings' they are.

Be serious about your customers' needs and expectations

"After a negative experience: 58% of customers will never use the company again – 58% will tell friends not to use the business – 16% would take revenge by posting a review online or sharing a poor experience on social media."
– NEWVOICEMEDIA

LEARNING STORY

At another time, I was asked to give one of our TLC (Think Like A Customer) Sessions to the employees of a company contracted by a big mining house. This was necessitated by two consecutive incidents of indifference and negative attitudes displayed as they served at the mine's canteen. Both incidents emanated from kitchen personnel not doing things in the way laid down and as expected by the customer. With a zero-tolerance on issues that brought harm or threatened the safety and health of everyone at the mine – the organisation had very strict rules, procedures and systems meant to ensure set standards would be met.

There was adequate induction, training and feedback, but the staff's attitudes took customer needs for granted - the incident's cost to the contractor and affected employees was huge. The chefs involved were asked to leave the canteen kitchen, the contractor had to look for replacements without affecting service delivery, had to incur costs of relocating and recruiting, whilst the contract's continuance was threatened.

Customers are the experts when it comes to knowing what is best for them and what their expectations are - never undermine their views and feedback.

THE LIMITERS OF SERVICE EXCELLENCE

Every individual and organisation must make it a priority to identify and eradicate anything that limits the provision of excellent service to customers. Sometimes it's the attitude of staff, policies that are suited for the organisation's own convenience or systems and processes that are not responsive to the needs and expectations of customers.

LEARNING STORY

A bus company whose luxury coach service I once used, takes the trophy for limiting excellent service.

Ironically, the company's pay off line and the promise they printed on their tickets, were the opposite of the service I experienced. They claimed to be a true travelling partner and a champion in serving customers. The service experience was so bad that my parting remarks with their bus driver was, *"Whoever owns this company is in serious trouble."*

Always Remember: Whenever there is discord or incongruence between what you promise the customer and what you practice, the customer will always go with what you do, as the real message - because that is what they see and experience.

Not surprisingly the icons on their ticket cover confirmed everything to be expected on the bus, *"Music, Climate control, Air Suspension, Reclining Seats, TV & Radio and Satellite Tracking"* – no mention of the care of customers. Indeed - the crew, office staff and operating systems did all they could to confirm the non-existence of a culture of service excellence.

My encounter with this bad service experience happened on my way back from running the first phase of a 5-day Customer Support and Service Delivery (CSSD) intervention for three municipal authorities, under our 5-Star Customer Service workshops. My car had broken down due to a malfunctioning engine sensor so I had to book a return bus to where I had left the car. I made my booking and paid my fare after the first day of training. Early in the morning of my return date, I got a call requesting me to attend another meeting, some 60km further from my original return destination.

What I thought was going to be a simple exercise of topping up my fare and adjusting my destination, ended up being one of the scariest experiences in customer service I have ever encountered. I literally get goose bumps when I think about that experience, even today.

I like to be organized, so I got to my training venue at the Holiday Inn and the first thing I did was to look up the number for the bus company offices in the city where I was training. I asked if the gentleman who answered could amend my booking so I dropped off at my new destination. I was told this was impossible. I insisted on knowing why, and the explanation was that, the company had no fare for the 60km distance between my booked return destination and the new one – I could not believe it! I pointed out that I felt this did not make any sense given there was a fare from where I was to my new destination – I suggested they just use the difference in fares to determine my top-up fare.

The answer was a simple, *"Sorry that is not possible. Maybe you can talk to our main office."* I called their main office and another gentleman answered. I relayed my story and I was asked why the guys where I was could not help. I explained that the system did not have a fare for my extended journey and the gentleman also had no clue how I could be helped. I suggested they cancel my original ticket and issue a new one, and the main office gentleman advised that I tell this to the team on the ground where I was.

With some hope, I called and offered my suggestion to cancel my ticket and issue a new one to my new destination – I was told that would be possible but it was going to attract a 20%

charge. We had an argument that I never won as I tried to point out that I did not want to cancel my booking or change the bus time, all I wanted was to extend my travel and give a bit more money to the company, and that I felt it was quite unfair to penalize me regardless of how small the amount seemed. I was bluntly told if I was not happy with that, then the only option was to find alternative transport. I had a meeting to attend, so I had to swallow my pride and advised I would come and get the adjustment effected.

After the training, I excused myself from having lunch with my hosts and the workshop participants, grabbed some packed lunch and rushed to the bus offices. When I got there, I was told I could not get the amendment effected as I was supposed to have done this, at least 4 hours before departure! For the third time, the third person I was dealing with referred to the company's *Terms and Conditions*. I was so shocked I couldn't shout or complain – I ended up smiling in disbelief. I asked what else could be done, I was told *"nothing"* and referred to a gentleman by the name, Steve.

Steve was a friendly and smiling gentleman, but still happy to be the fourth staff member to say, *"Well the company's Terms and Conditions do not give us room to do anything in such a case. Sorry, but you will have to drop off at your original destination and get alternative transport to your meeting."* My host company's training coordinator who had driven me to board the bus was equally shocked – what could we do? On reading through the over-quoted *Terms and Conditions*, not a single one of them covered my request to extend my journey or change my destination on the same bus and route.

I observed passengers who boarded without prior booking getting their tickets issued on board. The reason why this could not be done for me? – *"We have no fare for your trip extension"* – unbelievable! No one was empowered to adjust and issue a manual ticket for the difference.

I got onto the bus whilst planning the connecting logistics to my meeting. By the time we got to my destination I had made up my mind to engage the company's management regarding customer service. I then approached the cabin crew member and handed him a copy of our Customer Service participant workbook, politely asking him to forward it to their manager or the gentleman with whom I had a telephone conversation, and that I would contact the manager after the weekend. He refused and referred me to the driver who was outside. I approached the driver and made the same request – I did not expect to get the rude interrogation I got.

5-Star Customer Service

I was asked what the book was all about and why I wanted to send it. I explained the customer service handbook as well as related my experience that prompted me to engage management. I was told the manager would not be at the office, of which I politely asked him just to drop it off at the office. I was told, *"Hey you, take back your thing, whatever it is, we don't need it!"* Truthfully, the last time I was treated with disrespect the way this bus crew treated me, was at some minibus rank in my old neighbourhood in Egypt, Highfield Harare. Agitated by this attitude, I asked the bus crew if they really wanted to remain in business 5 years from that day. It was not like I was expecting to get an answer, because they did not care anyway.

This is the reason why I parted ways with them by remarking, *"Whoever owns this company is in serious trouble."* In a cut-throat market, like the transport industry in Zimbabwe, there will not be a place for such service providers, for long. A gentlemen who had accompanied a passenger and was also surprised by the conduct of the crew asked if he could take the rejected benefit of the handbook to his company – I gladly allowed him to collect the rejected *"thing."*

From the coach, claiming to be a champion in delivering service to customers, I took my bag and stood by the road side to catch a lift for the remaining 60km of my journey. Needless to say, I missed the first segment of my meeting – what a travelling partner I had! I was beginning to trust the bus company with the welfare and travel experience of my son to and from school. I cringed at the thought of what would happen to my son if there was a challenge that required responsiveness to customer needs from the service provider. You don't need to be a prophet to know what I did about that, and what kind of an example this experience will be during my workshops and the advice I will give to everyone in my circle of influence concerning choice of a traveling partner.

I was not even surprised when none of my four emails to the different email addresses on their website never got a response or acknowledgement of receipt.

Two critical issues come out of this learning story. Firstly, this is a typical case of systems and processes established for the convenience of the service provider and with no regard for the needs and expectations of customers. Secondly, affirmation of the research findings that showed, the major reason why most businesses lose customers being negative staff attitudes and indifference - where customers show disregard and little care for customers or their problems. Would it take a rocket scientist to explain the reason why other competitors, in the same industry, are sometimes fully-booked whilst others are almost always not full, even during pick-periods?

This would be a great place to remind each other, of the need to provide Excellent Service by understanding customer needs and expectations; then meeting those needs and exceeding expectations.

So when you aim to provide excellent service:

1. Seek first to understand what the needs of your customers are. Know who your customers really are.

2. Ask yourself, *"How would my customers define excellent service. What does it mean to them?"*

3. Process thoughts like: *"If I was the person on the other side of the counter, how would I want to be treated?"*

4. When you make decisions and put in place systems and policies, don't focus on what makes life easier for you in isolation to the impact of the decision on your customers. Always have the customer in mind – others call it, being *"customer-focused"* all the time and in our TLC Training Sessions we declare it - *"Think Like a Customer."*

Chapter 3

WHY SERVICE STANDARDS BECOME POOR

"Only 4% of customers will voice out their experience to the company after a bad experience."
                              -RUBY NEWELL-LEGNER

12 REASONS WHY SERVICE STANDARDS BECOME POOR

Make an effort to ensure that you are not found amongst those who contribute towards poor customer service.

1. **Customers who do not complain or commend**

   This segment of customers are uneducated on the importance of good customer service, even if they are learned people in their own area of specialty. Brushing aside the small service issues that matter, contributes towards falling service standards. Whenever you are not satisfied with the service provided, seek the next person in authority, and the next, and the next, until you get acceptable solutions or responses. Don't make some noise only when you are raising a complaint – also adopt a culture of making some music with your compliments whenever you receive excellent service; the world is already intoxicated from negative feedback.

2. A silent media

The untold stories of customers getting a raw deal when it comes to customer service delivery make service providers complacent. The media, in all its forms, need to continuously publicise both good and bad stories of customer service. This keeps service providers aware of the third eye watching them and the amplified customer-voice available to raise concern and highlight the negative impact of poor service. The *'free'* publicity that comes with exceptional stories of excellent service will become an incentive for service providers to deliver service excellence.

A media, silent on service matters, contributes towards poor service standards.

3. **Business managers and owners who do not appreciate they exist to meet customer needs, not just their own**

   We still have a fair share of service providers who influence a culture of bad service. The practice ends up being the standard for customer service personnel in their organizations. Culture is influenced from the top, therefore leaders and business owners need to lead by example.

4. **Business processes meant to make life easier for the business, at the expense of customers**

   Policies, procedures, forms and other business systems crafted by organizations without thinking about the customer, end up inconveniencing customers and reducing the quality of service experiences the customers receive. This includes times for tea breaks, lunch breaks or attendance of training by service providers leaving offices unmanned when customers visit for service. Type of forms used, language used, mode of communication as well as policies on returns, refunds and replacements, all make the list. Remember the, *"No Refund, No Returns, No Exchange"* signs in some shops? All of these, promote a poor service culture.

5. Misaligned strategic intents

Organisations that profess customer service on wall plaques, but adopting business practices and strategies that do not promote good customer service, need to change. The level of staff turnover, unavailability of adequate resources, work environments that are not conducive, all contribute towards limitations to excellent customer service delivery. This happens when core values publicised are in conflict with those practiced daily and experienced by customers during service transactions. Such misalignment leads to poor service standards.

6. Inconsistent practice and lack of training

There must be sustainability systems – customer service, like every other culture, needs to be reinforced, refreshed and re-communicated through training, induction programs, campaigns, competitions, reward ceremonies, publications and other tools. The absence of these systems will almost always limit the continuous improvement of customer service.

7. **An environment that creates a supplier's market**

    Monopoly of supply or service provision like the issuance of important documents, utility services like electricity and water, inter alia, will always contribute to poor quality of service provided to customers. Limited supply of goods and services or even too much buyer power (only one customer consuming a particular product), will all lead to complacency on the part of service providers. The monopoly mentality/attitude exposes customers to bad service, so competition will always be healthy, as it helps to improve customer service.

8. **Lack of advocacy groups - Non-existent or ineffective customer-representative groupings**

    Any market or area with a strong customer representative group always benefits, as service providers are always under pressure and scrutiny to ensure high standards of customer service. These associations must continue to present a common voice on behalf of customers and cater for the right to 5-Star customer service even for those customers who do not complain, for whatever reason.

9. Poor internal customer relations and processes

A work environment that is not harmonious will always make service providers indifferent towards customers. The resultant negative attitudes lead to blame games, where everyone doesn't want to take responsibility for promises made to customers.

10. Lack of initiative and focus

A lack of initiative and creativity on the part of service providers, means they quickly resign to say they cannot do anything to meet a customer's request. Service providers who lack a deliberate focus on meeting the needs and exceeding the expectations of customers, will always be limited in their ability to excel at customer service. Do not be limited by what the customer has asked for by name – identify the need and possible solutions within your policies and service offering, you will be amazed by the difference you can make.

11. Lack of continuous responsiveness to, and meaningful involvement of customers

There should be a genuine interest in understanding and responding to customer needs, requirements, suggestions and complaints. This one reason is the major factor why some parastatals or government agencies will not survive as privatised businesses. Without meaningful involvement of customers to understand their needs and what they expect, service providers will always miss the mark of excellence in pleasing customers.

12. Negative Staff Attitude

An attitude that does not care what customers think or say is the No. 1 enemy of 5-Star Customer Service. The best way to manage training and re-hiring costs is to hire employees who already possess a positive attitude.

THE COST OF BAD SERVICE

Consider the cost of not treating customers well. It is only exceptional customer service that can help you retain your existing customers and make those satisfied customers refer new business.

"13% of customers will tell 20 others about a bad experience."
- MERLIN

"91% of unhappy customers will not willingly do business with you again... It can take as much as 12 positive experiences to make up for 1 bad experience."
- RUBY NEWELL-LEGNER

"78% of customers have bailed on a transaction or not made an intended purchase because of a poor service experience... 70% were willing to spend more with companies they believe provide excellent customer service"
- AMERICAN EXPRESS SURVEY

"Reducing the loss of customers by 5% can increase your profitability by 25% to 125%."
LEADING ON THE EDGE OF CHAOS | EMMET & MARK MURPHY

HOW TO PROMOTE 5-STAR CUSTOMER SERVICE

Excellent Multiple Choices

Multichoice Africa, is a master at offering 'multichoices', convenience and responsiveness to consumers of their satellite TV services through DSTV. From an upper-tier service targeted to the high income-earners and the elite, their products and service offerings have continuously transformed to be excellently customised to cover the needs of all market segments served by a truly continental business.

5-Star Customer Service

Do You Only Listen To The Big Ones?
Covered under Star 3 on Communication Skills, is Sainsbury's Learning Story[3] of how one of their managers listened to the observations of a 3-year old. This led to them changing the name of one of their products, from Tiger bread to Giraffe bread. To go beyond expectations, not only did the manager reply in writing, but also sent a shopping gift card to the 3 year old customer. This is a great example of how to promote 5-Star Customer Service.

Not Just 'Another' Bus Company[4a]
ExtraCity Luxury Coaches is not just a passenger transport company. It is a service business highly focused on anticipating, identifying and responding to customer needs. The level of interaction between crew and passengers has built a loyal customer base as well as increased the opportunities for determining customer needs and expectations. The continuous development of off-board services in response to customer feedback, has made ExtraCity Luxury an excellent example of how 5-Star Customer Service is promoted.

The 'Foot-Scrubber' Boutique

My stories in this book will give you an idea of how much I travel on business. During one such trip, I had to go round an entire town looking for a foot-scrubber. After being referred to pharmacies without success, I ended up at a clothing boutique. They also did not have any scrubbers, but at least they asked me to check the following day. They delivered as promised.

I later learnt they never sold any foot scrubbers, but they went out of their way to get one from the market in one of the townships. Everyone else was comfortable to say they did not have what I was asking for. I ended up buying a shirt from that boutique.

I have already forgotten the name of the shop or the faces of the service providers, yet I still remember the experience and how important it made me feel.

10 THINGS THAT PROMOTE 5-STAR CUSTOMER SERVICE

1. Understanding Customer Needs and Expectations.

2. A Positive Attitude towards Customers and everything that concerns them.

3. Policies, Systems, Processes and Standards that are crafted with the customer in mind.

4. Customers who make their voice heard whenever they are not satisfied.

5. Customers who sing praises and take time to write or call to commend good service received.

6. Managers and leaders who lead by example in setting the standard for how customers must be treated.

7. Organisations that engrain the Customer Service element into their Mission, Values and Strategy.

8. Individuals who take PRIDE (Personal Responsibility In Delivering Excellence) during all customer encounters.

9. Continuous research on new and better ways to deliver quality memorable experiences to customers.

10. Becoming Extraordinary by doing the little Extra things which the Ordinary find excuses not to do.

LEARNING QUESTIONS

1. What else can you start doing within your organisation to promote 5-Star (Excellent) Customer Service?

2. Review your personal and organisation's service performance against the 12 Reasons Why Customer Service Standards Become Poor. Which areas do you need to start improving on, and how?

3. Assess your organisational performance against each of the 10 Things that Promote 5-Star Customer Service, and rate yourself on each aspect on a scale of 0-5 (0 being the worst and 5 the best).

4. From the results of the exercises above, list the areas that require improvement and come up with action plans, categorised into short term and long term priorities.

Chapter 4

KNOWLEDGE & SKILLS

"Education consists, not so much of knowledge, but of KNOWLEDGE EFFECTIVELY AND PERSISTENTLY APPLIED.

Men are paid, not merely for what they know, but more particularly for WHAT THEY DO WITH THAT WHICH THEY KNOW."

—HENRY FORD

It is important for service providers to know what is involved in customer service, and the skills they must possess in order to offer 5-Star Customer Service. The words of Henry Ford, quoted above, are a reminder that we prove how educated we are, by practicing the knowledge and skills we have acquired. This must be the aim of every customer service provider. In this chapter, we define those elements which everyone involved with internal and external customers, need to know. These are as basic as the simplified definitions of *'service'*, *'hospitality'* and *'excellent service,'* among other fundamental customer service principles.

The first thing to know is that, everyone who has a single customer is automatically in the service business, regardless of the sector of the economy they operate in. If you consider the statistics below – it pays to have competent people in the delivery of service to your customers. Continuous training and re-skilling of employees must be a top priority for every organisation that is serious about providing memorable experiences to its customers. Individuals must refine their skills in customer care and put them into practice with enthusiasm, on a daily basis – they must become Service Excellence Practitioners.

"78% of customers say that competent customer service representatives make them happy. 38 % say it's the personalization that keeps them coming back."
- MERLIN

"90% of customers will pay more to ensure a superior customer service."
- HARRIS INTERACTIVE/RIGHT NOW

CORPORATE STRATEGY

Every organisation's corporate strategy needs to reflect a deep understanding of the age of *"customer experience"* that we are living in.

- Do you know the principles that guide your organisation's customer service strategy and decisions?

- How clearly is your corporate strategy communicated to every member?

- Do you have a systematised way of providing memorable customer experiences?

WHAT IS SERVICE?

Service is ***"an action done to help somebody"*** or ***"work done for customers"***[5]

Examples include responding to customer requests like printing their account statement, opening the gate for them, passing salt to a colleague during lunch, helping a lost stranger with directions to where they are going or sending information required by the manager for a meeting. The list is endless and I hope you get the idea – anywhere we are, at any given time, we are surrounded by opportunities to provide service, whether at work, home or in-between.

CUSTOMER SUPPORT & SERVICE DELIVERY (CSSD)

Customer Service is divided into *Service Delivery, Customer Support* and *Customer Care*.

Service delivery is the actual performance of the requested action or the delivery of product or service offering required to meet customer needs. This refers to those tangible and intangible products customers expect the organisation to deliver, in response to their needs and expectations. Examples include availability of clean water running through their taps, electricity, meal prepared and served, salary paid and reflecting in account, goods or people transported from one point to the required destination or availing of connectivity to the internet or satellite signal.

Customer Support refers to the continuous responses given by service providers to the customers consuming their products and services so that the expected levels of satisfaction are sustained. This includes response to queries, resolution of complaints, repairs, service restoration, maintenance, upgrades and education on effective and efficient consumption of product or service benefit.

Customer Care cannot be sufficiently defined without going into what *Hospitality* is all about. This is because ***Hospitality is the element of Customer Service we refer to, as Customer Care***.

WHAT IS HOSPITALITY?

Hospitality can be defined as **'*the art of caring*'** – the kindness and friendliness extended to visitors, guests or strangers. This is demonstrated through the way we show genuine friendliness in welcoming them, taking care of their needs and making them feel comfortable and at home whenever they come into our own space.

This is the element of service that customers will always remember, long after the product or service paid for has expired, because it touches the customer's heart and emotions.

Hospitality shapes the memories of the service encounter – it creates the "Customer Experience."

Customer Experience

This is the total experience of product or service quality consumed and encountered by the customer and its relevance in meeting the underlying customer needs and expectations. When this is surrounded by an exceptional practice of *"the art of caring"*, it produces the Quality Memorable Customer Experiences referred to throughout this book and the related training sessions.

THE RELATIONSHIP BETWEEN SERVICE AND HOSPITALITY

The definitions of Service and Hospitality above, denote that as you do those things which help other people and as you meet their needs, whether through a tangible or intangible product; you need to serve them in a way which shows you care, that they are welcome in your environment and that you are going to do everything reasonably possible, to understand and satisfy their needs.

♦ In summary, you practice the *'art of caring'* in doing something that adds value to other people.

♦ Whilst *service is both an art and a science* – the caring part of customer service makes it more of an art (Customer Care) than it is a science (Service Delivery & Customer Support).

♦ Like with any other art, you cannot separate the artist from his or her art, which is why the human and attitude elements will remain key in determining the quality of customer service provided.

- As a science, the need to make quality of customer service measurable and predictable as well as move with technological advancements, continuous research and riding on systems and the information age train, will also remain key considerations for any serious service provider as they deliver their products and services.

- Customer care is an essential ingredient of good Customer service. Customer service is what we do or provide to meet customer needs. Customer care is how we do this.

- It is Customer Care that creates the Customer Experience enjoyed or endured by customers whenever they consume your products and services.

THE CUSTOMER IS KING

We have always heard that, *"the customer is king."* Why do we refer to the customer as king?

Customers bring the income which makes everyone and everything within the organisation to run. Without this revenue, businesses eventually close operations, employees lose their jobs and source of livelihood, whilst shareholders and investors forget about profits and eventually lose their capital. For this and more reasons – *the Customer is king.*

THE CUSTOMER IS KING

"There is only one boss, and whether a person shines shoes for a living or heads up the biggest corporation in the world, the boss remains the same. It is the customer! The customer is the person who pays everyone's salary and who decides whether a business is going to succeed or fail. In fact, the customer can fire everybody in the company from the chairman (CEO) on down, and he can do it simply by spending his money somewhere else.

Literally everything we do, every concept perceived, every technology developed and associate employed, is directed with this one objective clearly in mind – pleasing the customer."
—SAM M. WALTON | WAL-MART

Love them, listen to them, respond to their needs and your business will grow - benefits and profits will increase.

THE CUSTOMER SATISFACTION FORMULA

- ♦ How do you ensure your level of customer service brings satisfaction to your customers?

Understanding Customer Needs
+
Understanding Customer Expectations
+
Customer Service Performance
+
Customer Care (Hospitality)
=
CUSTOMER SATISFACTION

Adding the little "extra" elements to this formula will enable the creation of pleasant memorable experiences required for 5-Star Customer Service attainment. 5-Star Customer Service is about going beyond Customer Satisfaction:

5-STAR CUSTOMER SERVICE
=
Thinking Like Your Customers
(Empathise/Put yourself in their shoes)
+
Offering Memorable Experiences
(Care enough to touch their heart/emotions)
+
Performing to Exceed Expectations
(Going the extra mile & executing with Excellence)

EVEN IN CUSTOMER SERVICE & HOSPITALITY, **KNOWLEDGE IS THE GREATEST SOURCE OF CONFIDENCE**

LEARNING STORY – THE EXTRACITY LUXURY WAY[4b]

ExtraCity Luxury Coaches embraced these customer service principles and strove to make them a part of their culture. When two large competitor companies merged their operations to strengthen their competition in the routes covered by ExtraCity, they were soon to learn that *"the customer is king"* and that *"service is the only difference that makes a difference when there is no difference."* The competitors put newer coaches with superior product features and amenities, charged the same fares and even went on to head hunt a few employees from ExtraCity.

The competitors were forced to withdraw their service within a month of launching an offensive, simply because customers chose to remain loyal to ExtraCity – the kings had spoken and the difference came from the service they were receiving, not the equipment features or price. Instead of investing in fancy features on their buses, the ExtraCity management instead chose to invest in improving their crew members' knowledge of customer service to further improve the customer experiences their customers were receiving on every trip.

As we always say in Zimhost and Afrihost workshops, ***"Service is the only difference that*** *can make a difference when there is no difference."* Tony Hsieh, CEO of Zappos.com confirms in his book, *"Delivering Happiness - A Path to Profits, Passion and Purpose,"* that everything else like price and product features can be copied and replicated overnight – the ultimate distinction remains the quality of customer service attached to the products or services offered.

LEARNING STORY

- How does a company enter into a highly competitive market, and within a short period of time dominated the route they serve, growing the fleet of coaches from just one vehicle to over 20 luxury coaches?

- How has it been possible to fend off aggressive attempts by competitors to dislodge the growing dominance?

For ExtraCity Luxury Coaches, the answer has been simple – *"Focus on the things that cannot be copied because we are not just a bus company, but a service business. Our continuous homework is to respond to the needs of our customers"* This is the view of the company's directors. After pressing Dave and Fari Masimira to be more elaborate, what I learnt from this growing player in the competitive transport industry, included the following:

1. Their choice of route was largely influenced by listening to their drivers and hosting crew. **(Listen to members of your team)**

2. All their developmental initiatives and expansion programs have been in response to expressed customer needs and requests. **(Listen to your customers and respond to their needs and expectations)**

3. They have adopted a system of delivering the service to customers. **(Systematise customer service into the daily practices of your business)**

4. They are continuously looking for ways to deliver quality customer experiences so as to make their brand unique. **(Continuously improve your organisation's systems, methods and policies in line with customer needs)**

5. They practically demonstrate how they care for their team members, even beyond the work place. **(Build a team, show you care and work as a family unit)**

6. They invest in training and development of staff and management. **(Your organisation is only as good as its people – take staff and management development seriously)**

7. The directors personally go out of their way to directly get feedback from their customers and to experience the same service they offer to others. They deliberately park their cars and travel on their coaches. **(Literally, put yourself in the customers' shoes – feel what they feel, experience what they experience and adjust your service accordingly)**

CUSTOMERS ARE ALWAYS RIGHT...EVEN WHEN THEY ARE WRONG!

Remember - Never argue with customers, because *"the customer is always right."*

- They must always retain honour and respect, regardless of what the facts state – don't let them lose face.

- Their *"unreasonable"* demands can be positively used to consider new opportunities to meet current and future needs.

- If you win an argument with a customer and lose their business, have you really won?

- Don't let your ego get in the way of professional business conduct. Growing in self-control and other Emotional Intelligence attributes, is necessary for 5-Star Customer

Service providers – especially, when the facts and circumstances are tempting enough to prove you are right and the customer is wrong. Beware the trap.

- Use the Toolbox approach and available official channels, in a professional way, to remain covered and protected from abuse and possible penalties or litigation.

COMPETENCES OF A 5-STAR CUSTOMER SERVICE PROVIDER

1. **Service Excellence Knowledge**
   To be effective in providing service, develop knowledge of the following:

   a) Important developments within your organisation.

   b) Strategic direction, policies, rules & regulations essential to product and service delivery.

   c) The nature and category of your customers and their needs/expectations.

   d) People and departments responsible for key functions that help and support your service performance.

   e) Professional Service Excellence language, systems and processes.

2. Service Excellence Skills

Acquire and practice the skills below:

a) Service and Hospitality skills – Welcoming, greeting, friendliness, helpfulness.

b) Planning, organizing and analytical skills.

c) Professional methods of complaint handling and resolution.

d) Team building skills, effective inter-departmental support.

e) Communication skills – Interpersonal, face-to-face, telephone, email, social media, listening, non-verbal, vocal & verbal skills.

f) Emotional Intelligence – Self-awareness, self-control, social awareness, relationship management & positive attitude.

g) Job-specific technical competences and qualifications – Skills and expertise required to deliver quality products and services, most importantly, aiming for 'practitioner-status.'

3. **Service Excellence Values & Attitude**

Values are the guiding principles through which you make important decisions. It is easier and more effective to sustain a positive attitude when your professional conduct is values-based. Add-on to the non-exhaustive values and attitudes below:

a) Develop a sense of Care and PRIDE.

b) Always appreciate the needs of your customers.

c) Recognize your own prejudices and develop a non-judgmental acceptance of others.

d) Show empathy for those you serve.

e) Exude the Spirit of Excellence that goes beyond the expected, whilst paying attention to detail.

f) Love what you do and practice with professional passion.

g) Be respectful and courteous at all times.

KNOW HOW TO DEAL WITH "DIFFICULT CUSTOMERS"

Practicing 5-Star Customer Service knowledge, skills, values and attitude, equips you with the ability to effectively handle even the so-called *'difficult customers.'*

1. Those whose demands seem to go beyond the reasonable.
2. Those you don't know how to please.
3. Those who just enjoy being *"difficult"* or *"unreasonable"*

Whilst you cannot change the customer's or another person's attitude, you can choose to have a say in how you respond to the negative attitude shown to you.

DEAL WITH COMPLAINTS PROFESSIONALLY

"The problem is not the problem; the problem is your attitude about the problem"
- VIKTOR E. FRANKL

"41% of customers say that getting their issues resolved quickly is the most important aspect of good customer service"
- INFINITContact

"Resolve a complaint in the customer's favour and they will do business with you again 70% of the time."
-LEE RESOURCES

The Need for Mutual Respect

In as much as service providers must respect customers, there is also a need for customers to show respect for those serving them. This is key in building lasting relationships between customers and service providers. Respect, especially when it's mutual, becomes the oil that lubricates the customer service engine.

Respond to disrespect in a professional way

In one of the banks, a story is told, of a prominent gentleman who approached a teller to cash-in his cheque. The teller asked for his identification documents, according to procedure. The egocentric gentleman is said to have quipped, *"Hey young man, don't you have a television set at your house?"* (This was to drive the point that he was always on local TV news and everyone was supposed to know him!) During those days satellite TV (DSTV) was a preserve for the elite. The teller, having a bad attitude for a service provider, hit back, *"Sir, I'm not sure, but on which channel of DSTV do you feature?"*

The issue did not just end at the branch manager's desk or the CEO's office, it reached the board chairman! In most cases, such customers are the easiest to please – if they want you to *"feel their status"* then just *"feel them,"* you will become good friends. You will not lose much, but will save yourself unnecessary trouble. Just guard against abusive conduct and deal with it appropriately.

- Again – remember, The Toolbox/Recipe Approach covered in earlier Chapters. Use a respectful, positive attitude to select the required ingredients for that particular recipe!

- Whenever in doubt or overwhelmed by the situation – consult with or refer to the next person in authority.

Know When To Draw the Line – Be Assertive and Respectful

There are instances when you may decide it better to lose the custom, than to do something that will jeopardize both the customer's interests as well as your own, personally and professionally. A customer insisting on a wrong medical procedure or an illegal intervention to solving their problem, are not a good excuse for justifying bad business practice in the name of service excellence and the principle of empathy.

If you are diligent enough in looking at their actual needs, at that point in time they might not be in need of your expertise – they might, first and foremost, be in need of counselling expertise more than anything else. A skilled professional service provider should be able to respectfully communicate a negative response, giving the reasons and offering some advice if in a position to give sound advice, otherwise refer to someone who can do so. You might lose the financial transaction, but you have made an investment into your market-integrity account.

LEARNING STORY - THE ABUSIVE CUSTOMER

During my days as a Retail Banking manager, I returned to the office one day to find my secretary in shock and disturbed by the racial abuse that one of our customers had just offloaded on her.

The customer service officer and the operations manager had tried, for a couple of days, to get the client in question to regularise their overdrawn account to avoid any cheques getting unpaid and referred back to the drawer. When the team failed to get the requested cooperation, one or two cheques were not honoured by the bank, understandably causing the customer some embarrassment.

When the angry customer called the bank and could not find me, he left a message with my secretary, but the language used included words I cannot even get printed in this book. The racially abusive words were not even touching on the issue at hand, they were describing what the customer thought of me as a person, my team members and the bank I worked for.

I composed myself, picked up the phone and returned the call. I objectively summarised how the issue in question had unfolded until it got to the decision to return the cheques. The customer could not offer suggestions as to how they felt I could have handled the situation any better. I then firmly but respectfully advised that any form of abuse thrown at me or my team would not be acceptable. Lastly, I intimated our commitment to serve all our clients professionally but that we were prepared to lose his business if it meant receiving such unwarranted abuse. I left the bank many years ago, we remain in very good books with the client and he still does business with the same bank!

5-Star Customer Service

Chapter 5

BACK2BASICS

"On a global scale, less than 6% of customers find businesses exceeding their expectations."
- MERLIN

ALWAYS BEGIN WITH THE CUSTOMERS' NEEDS

I am not always accurate when reciting all the five or seven Ps of a marketing strategy, but I have never forgotten the basic principle, that the whole process must start with the identification of the needs of the target market.

This same principle is a fundamental law of providing 5-Star Customer Service. If you are going to please your customers, you must first invest in understanding their needs and expectations. The KYC (Know Your Customer) exercises must move from being mere legal or regulatory requirements, to become essential tools in providing exceptional and personalised customer service experiences. Knowing the customer does not end with asking them to complete forms, submit pictures of themselves or such other requirements. It is knowing them personally and individually, what they think and how they expect to be served.

It is appreciating them in their own world, understanding what affects them and their business, asking them the right questions and making meaningful conversations that help you understand them better.

FORMULA FOR GROWTH

> *"Over the years, the number one driver of our growth at Zappos has been repeat customers and word of mouth. Our philosophy has been to take most of the money we would have spent on paid advertising and invest it into customer service and the customer experience instead, letting our customers do the marketing for us through word of mouth."*
> - TONY HSIEH | DELIVERING HAPPINESS

In what I call the *Mathematics of Customer Service*, the formula for growth is depicted through the simple equation:

GROWTH

=

Retention of Existing Customers

+

Attraction of New Customers

LEARNING QUESTIONS

1. What customer service initiatives can you introduce in your department or organisation, to improve the level of customer satisfaction, starting from today?

2. How can you contribute towards the growth of your organisation?

3. What strategies can you put in place, to retain key internal and external customers?

4. How can you start using 5-Star service principles to attract new customers as well as the best internal customers?

WHAT THE BEST IN THE WORLD ARE DOING[6]

Only notable companies have provided a practical demonstration of the formula for growth, in the way it has been done by the online retailer, Zappos.com. After growing from no revenue to over US$1 billion in annual sales in less than 10 years, Zappos.com ended up being acquired by Amazon in a deal worth US$1.2 billion. In his book, *"Delivering Happiness,"* Tony Hsieh shares important principles that shaped the organisation's culture and gave momentum to the phenomenal growth Zappos.com has experienced. According to Tony, these are key indicators to what can help organizations retain existing customers as well as attract new ones.

Some of the initiatives included:

1. Making customer service the responsibility of the entire company – not just one department or a few selected employees.

2. Focusing on organisation culture as No. 1 priority.

3. Applying knowledge and skills gathered on providing pleasant experiences, to the way the business is run.

4. Helping employees to grow, both personally and professionally.

5. Having a passion to make a positive difference in the world around the organisation and its people.

In the words used by Tony, is the secret revealed,

"Even though it would hurt our growth, we decided to cut most of our marketing expenses, and refocused our efforts on trying to get the customers who had already bought from us to purchase again and more frequently. Little did we know that this was actually a blessing in disguise, as it forced us to focus more on delivering better customer service. In 2003, we would decide to make customer service the focus of the company... at the time, our number one priority wasn't customer service. It was simply survival."

– TONY HSIEH | DELIVERING HAPPINESS

- If your No. 1 priority is *"simply survival"* – it might be time to re-focus and take some notes from Tony Hsieh and Zappos.com.

- Invest in improving your service culture – that is where your source of revenue resides.

- Personalised customer service is now a standard market expectation. Customers are different – they have unique needs and expectations.

- 5-Star Customer Service means personalising and customising your products and services to meet those needs and exceed the expectations.

THE EXCELLENCE (5-STAR) FACTOR

"On a global scale, less than 6% of customers find businesses exceeding their expectations."
- MERLIN

Excellence is measured by brilliance, distinction, superior quality and is determined by the little extra things that influence the difference, between the ordinary and the extra-ordinary. This is the same principle which applies to the difference between good, expected and excellent service or what in this book and in our training workshops, we refer to as, *"5-Star Customer Service."*

A 5-Star rating is a Mark of Excellence

In this Chapter, we consider different principles you can adopt and practice, to help you attain 5-Star Customer Service status. With less than 6% of customers finding businesses exceeding their expectations, you need to increase practice of the little extra things which ordinary service providers do not want to do. That may find you as one of those counted amongst 5-Star Service providers.

"Whatever you do, do it well. Do it so well that when people see you do it, they will want to come back and see you do it again, and they will want to bring others and show them how well you do what you do."

- WALT DISNEY

Chapter 6

UNDERSTAND YOUR CUSTOMERS

"You don't know customers, until you respond to their needs. You cannot respond to their needs, unless you know them"
— ARCHIBALD MARWIZI

Remember: *Everyone or every business that has a customer, is in the Service business regardless of the economic sector they operate in.*

Understanding your customers is a vital component in positioning yourself to meet their needs and exceeding their expectations.

Let's simply define **Customers as,** *those people or organizations that depend on you to meet their needs.* If these people fall outside the employment of your organisation, they are referred to as *'external customers'* and those from within, as *'internal customers.'* You can then extend the same principle and apply it to a customer service view of your home/family or community set-up. Everywhere around you, whether at work or outside the work environment, are customers – people depending on you to help them meet their diverse needs.

1. INTERNAL CUSTOMERS

Internal Customers can also be called Supporting or Support Customers and they include your Subordinates, Supervisors as well as your work mates. They all deserve and expect 5-Star Customer Service from you and your organisation.

a) **Supporting Internal Customers**

These include Subordinates, Supervisors/Managers and Work mates.

2. EXTERNAL CUSTOMERS

External Customers are not directly employed by, or a part of your organisation. They can be further split into Consuming, Supplying, Investing and Facilitating Customers.

a) Consuming Customers

These are regular or adhoc customers who consume or enjoy your products and services for a payment or not.

b) Supplying Customers

You actually pay these customers for the support service they provide to enable you to better serve the consumers of your own products and services.

LEARNING STORY

Many years ago, when I worked for a large insurance company, part of my responsibilities included calculating and paying the commission due to all the insurance brokers we dealt with. During one of the meetings with the director and senior management of one insurance broker, I grew to appreciate that the cheque from our company was probably the largest source of income for most of the broker companies.

This understanding changed my approach to the way I handled this portfolio. I started working with them to ensure all employee contributions and file submissions were up-to-date, to enable the smooth processing of commission due to them. Sometimes it meant seeking special authority to issue the odd cheque when it failed to meet the set deadlines. These brokers ensured business and revenue continued coming to the employee benefits business and they were key partners to the company. The least we could do, was to support them by ensuring efficient payment of commission, whenever it was due.

LEARNING QUESTIONS

1. How are you serving your supplying customers?

2. If you were one of your suppliers – would you enjoy doing business with your organisation?

SUPPLIERS' INDUCTION

A retail pharmacy manager with one of our clients in the medical services sector, expressed her frustration with supplying customers not fully appreciating the impact of their service on their customer service value-chain. My recommendation was for them to introduce a suppliers' induction program.

This gives you the opportunity to provide suppliers with all the important information regarding your needs and expectations. They will have a clearer picture of where their own service fits-in, how it affects your business and impact on your customers. This approach has been effectively used at Zappos.com, where they view their suppliers as important business partners. Without reliable and responsive suppliers, your promise to provide 5-Star Customer Service will always be difficult to keep. Help them understand your business, your needs and your customers.

There is room for 5-Star Customer Service in those Finance, Administration and Accounts departments. Information and the practice of courtesy will always help suppliers to plan and feel respected, even when you end up failing to pay them, when you said you would. Don't wait for them to complain, but you must proactively engage them.

c) Supporting External Customers

- Family & Friends
- Clubs & Professional Associations

In what ways can you provide 5-Star Customer Service to your family, friends and to the organisations you are a member of?

d) Investing Customers

Shareholders and other Investors need and expect return on their investment, in the same way that management and staff expect their perks. They require information and other disclosure expectations.

- How well are you serving the needs of your investing customers?

e) Financing/Funding Customers

These include Financial Institutions and other funders.

- Can your financiers trust you to do what you promised you would?
- Do you understand their needs, and how much have you been able to meet or exceed their expectations?

f) Facilitating Customers

The examples of facilitating customers include the Communities and Environment you operate within, Regulatory Authorities and related stakeholders.

5-Star Customer Service

- Discuss and define the needs and expectations of your various facilitating customers?

- List some ways you can start providing 5-Star Customer Service to this category of customers.

TECHNIQUES FOR UNDERSTANDING CUSTOMER NEEDS

Customers are different, they have unique needs – TLC means customizing your approach to each customer and customer experience. Being timely, means something different to a semi-literate old lady who needs help to complete some forms, to what it means to a young executive in a rush to make it to their next business meeting in time.

1. Ask the right questions and allow customers to guide you to the answers.

2. Frequent interaction with customers, especially in their own environment, will enable you to see what affects them, what drives them and how you can add value to them.

3. Conduct research and surveys to keep up with market dynamics and changing customer needs.

4. Seek customer feedback after any interaction with customers or after any changes effected to your products and services.

5. Walking in their shoes can also mean joining in the queues they stand in, and consuming the same services you provide them with.

If you take time to understand your customers' present needs, you can grow your capacity to anticipate their future requirements.

CUSTOMERS

"You don't know them until you respond to their needs. You cannot respond to their needs unless you know them."
— A.T. MARWIZI

Chapter 7

THE INGREDIENTS FOR 5-STAR CUSTOMER SERVICE

"By 2020, customer experience will overtake price and product as the key brand differentiator."
- CUSTOMERS 2020 REPORT

PRACTICE THE GOLDEN RULE

The root of the principles of empathy and TLC (Think Like a Customer), is the Golden Rule:

"Do to/for others what you would also want done to/for you"

It is from this, that every individual serving customers must understand the need to *"put themselves into the customer's shoes"* or as others put it, *"stand in another's moccasin or leather and walk a mile in their shoes."* Every time you encounter a customer, there is need to constantly Think Like you were that Customer (TLC).

This must make a service provider reflect on their encounter with customers, by processing what I call (In my book - ***It's My Life***) "*Golden-rule thoughts*" like:

- If I was the one requesting this service, how would I want to be treated or greeted?

- If the patient I am serving was my own mother, how would I want other medical personnel to treat her?

- If there was a burst sewer line on my door step, how swiftly would I want service providers to respond and resolve the problem?

- If I was the one not understanding certain business requirements and procedures, how would I want to be assisted?

- If I was old, illiterate or physically challenged, how would I want to be treated and served? What facilities would I need to suit my needs?

You can add more questions relevant to your line of work and business, to help you reflect on and visualize the TLC concept at work.

LEARNING STORY

I lost an argument with my phone one day and found myself in a long queue to get my phone line unblocked – I had entered the wrong PIN code for more than the number of attempts permitted, because I insisted there was no way I could forget a code I had used for so many years! No sooner had I started fidgeting because I am allergic to queues, did a Customer Service supervisor in my telephone service provider's shop approach clients to manage the growing queue. It seemed like she was reading our minds because we had just mentioned amongst ourselves as customers, how someone needed to do something about the queue.

Explaining that she also did not want to be made to stand in long queues for service, she went on to ask everyone, one by one, how they needed to be assisted. In no time, she had referred people to respective desks for assistance, whilst for people like me, she quickly issued some forms to complete and in no time our service was restored. She thought like someone who was *"allergic to queues!"*

LEARNING QUESTIONS

♦ What are you doing for your customers that reflects your understanding of the TLC principle?

♦ Are you not guilty of putting your customers through the very things you do not want to go through when you go elsewhere for service?

♦ What *"Golden-rule thoughts"* can you start asking yourself and your team members, to improve the way you respond to customer needs?

Think Like a Customer!

OFFER PLEASANT MEMORABLE EXPERIENCES

"By 2020, customer experience will overtake price and product as the key brand differentiator."
- CUSTOMERS 2020 REPORT

"After a positive customer experience: 76% would recommend the company to others while 51% would use the business more frequently."
- NEWVOICEMEDIA

5-Star Customer Service

The statistics above, augment the non-negotiable global thrust and positioning of the *"customer experience"* factor in business and service delivery.

Customers will, at times, forget the name of a product or the price they paid for a service, but will always remember the experience they had in the process of consuming the product or service. The reason being that, they would have attached an emotion or feeling of their experience to that product - the feeling will remain engraved in the memory long after the service or product has expired.

One of the Best Global Brands, Coca Cola, has gone further with this, by researching on their customers' most popular names and any other words they could be emotionally attached to, and printing those words and names on the containers of the Coca Cola products. These are simple initiatives, but they offer a personalised experience with a product, going beyond just the consumption of the cola beverage. And we all wonder, what is the secret behind *"the world's best-selling non-essential product?"*[7]

LEARNING QUESTIONS

Every individual and organisation, serious about providing 5-Star Customer Service, must answer these questions:

1. How do your customers feel about the way you are currently treating them?

2. How do you want them to feel about your service?

3. What memories would make them remember your service all the time, and make them want to return?

4. How can you begin to give them those memories and feelings?

5. Why do you want them to feel that way or hold on to those memories?

This element of Service Excellence is about offering unforgettable experiences to help promote loyalty and repeat business. This can be achieved through various ways.

5-Star Customer Service

A) PROVIDE UNIQUE PRODUCT/SERVICE OFFERINGS

One place guaranteed of a visit whenever I am in Victoria Falls is The Boma Restaurant. They only serve one meal a day – that dinner! It's not just about the food and drink. The whole package is a well-choreographed experience, with everything purposefully set to attach feelings and memories about the service. I don't remember the manager's name, the waiters' names or even the price I paid last time I was there, except that it was way above the average dinner cost in places around.

I still vividly remember the experience, how it made me feel and how I wouldn't mind going back again and again. For sure, I have taken my family and every group I have trained in the Victoria Falls has had at least one dinner night at The Boma.

The way you are greeted at the main entrance and have a Chilenje cloth tied around your neck as they explain the dressing, you get an option for a group photo as you enter, table already prepared, you get to enjoy the African appetizers and starters using traditional cutlery, the lesson and demonstration of traditional dances and what they mean, the roast meat or game for the day on the huge fire, the option for photos of the whole evening put on

5-Star Customer Service

a disk, the buffet with choice of fresh meats for braai as you wait, the big heat-preserving steel plates, participation in a percussion band with each guest playing their own drum under leadership of the band leader, joining into the Boma Party, dancing to the drums inside a circle as other guests cheer you on. Now that's a well-crafted experience, executed with excellence. You could remember that for decades.

The story of Parama bread in the city of my birth, needs no introduction to those who lived there in the late 90s. The bread was so good, fresh and tasty that for the first time as a teenager, I could finish a loaf of bread on my own. I do not remember the number of times I had to walk from school to our home, some 5km away, just to be able to buy half a loaf of bread and eat on my long walk home.

The competition had no answer to this offering, to the extent that some of them started intimidating the public by peddling rumours that this bakery and its bread were popular because black magic was being used to lure customers. This did not discourage us from looking for no other loaf besides the Parama bread!

- ♦ How do you craft your own script, in your line of business?

♦ How can you make your product or service so outstanding and excellent for its purpose, that the market will beat the path to your place and want that taste or experience repeatedly?

"If you're not doing some things that are crazy, then you're doing the wrong things."
                                            -LARRY PAGE, CO-FOUNDER - GOOGLE

♦ What disruptive ideas are you working on, for the benefit of your organisation and its customers?

B) BE RESPONSIVE TO THE NEEDS AND REQUESTS OF YOUR CUSTOMERS

My definition of a holiday has always meant one spent and enjoyed with family or friends. After responding to a quiz that appeared in one of the weekly newspapers, I won a weekend for two, at the 5-Star Meikles Hotel in Harare. When I raised an issue that, for me, it would not really be fun if we left our children (we had two back then) at home. The hotel got back to me within a few minutes to advise they would add a complimentary adjoining room for the children. We enjoyed the free weekend as a family.

That kind of responsiveness made it an experience to remember, even my wife talks about it time and again. The last time I hosted a foreign investor in Harare, it did not take any deep thought for me to use the Meikles Hotel for both accommodation and the meetings we had.

A good product is not enough if you are not responsive to customers' needs and expectations. This was proven by a newly opened supermarket in a major city. Of all the things that started attracting people to this new supermarket, was their fresh and tasty bread. It was like experiencing the resurrection of the Parama loaf that I mentioned earlier. Queues started growing as people waited for this tasty mass of flour and other ingredients, especially after 5pm as most people left their offices to go home.

The queues grew longer and people became more impatient each day, to the point where a shelf window on the bakery section got smashed during one of the skirmishes to grab a loaf. I tried to raise the issue with the bakery staff but I seemed to be talking *gibberish*. I then had a chat with one of the managers, raising concern about the poor planning and service being given, especially where the bread was concerned. The next two times my wife and I tried to get bread on separate occasions we each had to wait for close to 30 minutes. This time around, the bread was available on the shelves, but still you had to join a long queue to get it sliced.

Slowly we started going back to our old supermarket with a less tasty loaf, but offering the convenience, respect and responsiveness we expect to get as paying customers. We had trusted them with our appetites but they disappointed us and ended up betraying our taste buds. Whenever you treat customers like this, they end up voting with their feet and wallets.

WHAT THE BEST IN THE WORLD ARE DOING

The following letter appeared in a national daily newspaper, under the *"Letters to the Editor"* section. The letter was titled, ***"Hats off to ExtraCity bus service management."***

"I would like to commend the management of ExtraCity bus service for the valiant efforts made in the provision of daily transport services.

The fleet of buses plying the Bulawayo-Hwange-Victoria Falls route have eased transport blues faced by residents owing to poor services provided by the National Railways of Zimbabwe trains that failed to arrive in Bulawayo and Harare on time.

Nowadays most people travel on a single day from Victoria Falls to either Bulawayo or Harare. However, I have noted with great concern that there are no plug-in points to recharge cellphones for passengers on board.

It should be taken into consideration that it is important for passengers on board to communicate with their loved ones.

I therefore, appeal to the ExtraCity Bus Service management to install plug-in points close to passenger seats so that passengers have access to the cellphone recharging sockets.

I hope my submission will be taken into consideration."[4b]

A couple of months after this letter appeared in the newspaper, I passed through the ExtraCity offices and the management was looking for contact details of the customer who wrote the letter. Not only did they want to appreciate the feedback with a grocery hamper, they wanted to advise the customer that they had taken delivery of four new coaches. All the new coaches had been fitted with a cellphone battery charging socket for each passenger. Now, that is what I call 5-Star response to customer needs and requests!

LEARNING QUESTIONS

1. What issues make customers turn away from your great product or service? Can you identify the ones that seem like *'petty issues'* to the extent you might even overlook them?

5-Star Customer Service

2. How responsive are you to customers' feedback and concerns?
3. In what ways have you prepared yourself to satisfy the expectations of the volumes of customers you are likely to attract?

C) SHOW CREATIVITY IN SOLVING PROBLEMS

During a two week break-away session in Victoria Falls, to cover a specialized training program for a corporate client, we had to split the participants into two groups, each coming for a week. Our program had indoor programs up to lunch time and thereafter outdoor afternoon and evening activities. Each group would spend the first 3 days at The Kingdom Resort and the last 2 days at The Elephant Hills Hotel, with the change in environment intended to improve the learning experience. We had worked on this program and made relevant bookings, including payments, a few months before we started.

After the first 3-day program at The Kingdom, we moved to Elephant Hills for the final leg of our program. Upon checking-in, we were told the hotel was fully occupied, meaning someone had somehow double-booked some of our reserved rooms. There was another conference which had increased demand for accommodation. The hotel tried to convince us to move back to The Kingdom Resort, but we politely refused, suggesting instead, that they move whoever they had given the rooms we had paid for months in advance. We went ahead with our training activities, whilst we left them to solve the problem.

A few check-outs later, we were advised that we were now two rooms short. We insisted every one of us was going to stay in the same place, just like we had deliberately planned.

The very friendly gentlemen I ended up talking to, was the general manager, who was quick to apologise for the inconvenience, before advising that he had no option but to seek authority for the solution he had in mind. We went ahead with a few remaining activities, including crossing into Zambia and Botswana for activities that afternoon and we left him to do what he had in mind.

When we returned to check into our rooms and freshen up, we were advised that I was going to be using the Presidential Suite and my co-facilitator would be given the next best suite at the same rates we had paid. That arrangement stayed for the duration of our stay into the weekend as we waited to join the next group at The Kingdom on the Sunday. Problem solved - with a bit of creativity and going the extra mile.

Each line of business has its unique ways and opportunities for creative resolution to challenges that affect the quality of service expected by customers.

LEARNING QUESTIONS

1. Instead of saying *"sorry, there is nothing we can do,"* how else can you solve customers' complaints within the policy framework of your organisation?

2. What else can you do to empower your staff and enable the exploration of different options in creating solutions for customers?

3. Do you have a system in place to help this process?

Remember - the key is to always remain within your power and authority to act. Whenever in doubt or the issue goes beyond you – always refer to the next person in authority.

D) ADOPT A GENUINE PERSONAL APPROACH

Service experiences are more of an art, than they are a science. You cannot separate the service from the person providing it – the service carries a part of its provider's personality and attitude. That personal touch gives the difference when the product, the quality or the price,

5-Star Customer Service

are the same - when everything else that can be copied has been replicated. This personalised or customised art of caring, is the component of service that cannot be copied.

All your competitors can announce the next moment that they are *ISO 9001:2015-Certified* like you, but the Personal Touch can only be *Customer-Certified*. No matter how similar the services may seem, the DNA of each brand will remain unique to that personal or organisational brand.

I have been invited to a number of events in different sectors, including church organizations, colleges and schools, but in no other had I encountered an experience of a genuine personal approach to hospitality as I did at Celebration Church. It should have been in 2002, yet I still have pleasant memories up to now. I had been invited to attend the special Fathers' Day church service for that year.

I can still visualize the first few people I met by the entrance, in their maroon blazers and black trousers and skirts. The way I was greeted, welcomed, ushered inside and to my seat. I was not invited as a speaker or a VIP guest at all, but the way I was treated made me feel like one. I could not stay for the cake and tea offered to me and others who had visited or attended church for the first time as I had to rush for another meeting.

This is not to say all the other churches and organizations I have been invited to or gone to, are not genuine or personal in their hospitality – it was just the difference in the way these important service aspects were expressed and demonstrated at this particular church, and on this particular day, that made lasting impressions on my memory. I do not remember what the Pastor spoke about that day, but I still remember how the reception I got made me feel.

LEARNING QUESTIONS

1. How genuinely friendly are you, in your welcome greeting or smile whenever you encounter people?

2. What else can help attach the element of a personal touch to your service, whilst you remain within the generally acceptable boundaries of professional business or social conduct?

Always remember that a genuine smile comes from the heart, not just the act of your facial muscles pulling on your lips to expose the teeth (in my case both the teeth and gums!).

Touch the heart - Appeal to Emotions – Share the Enthusiasm

"70% of buying experiences are based on how the customer feels they are being treated."
- MCKINSEY

- Service becomes 5-Star or excellent, when it is outstanding and superior to the ordinary or usual standard. It has to be of a very high quality.

- As Aristotle said, *"We are what we repeatedly do. Excellence then is not an act, but a habit."* This must become a habit, a way of doing things - a culture.

LEARNING QUESTIONS

1. How close are you to your customers?

2. What are your innovative ideas for connecting and networking with your customers?

3. How much of your strategy is influenced by input from your customers?

4. In what ways are you striving to be the best customer service provider in your sector?

E) GO THE EXTRA-MILE – BE EXTRA-ORDINARY

"Do you see a man who excels in his work? He will stand before kings; he will not stand before unknown man"
- THE HOLY BIBLE

We stated earlier, that for service to be excellent, it has to be superior or outstanding. Most of the time, this means going beyond the set standards. The difference between the words *'ordinary'* and *'extra-ordinary'* is the little *'extra'* added to the *'ordinary'*.

When two things are both ordinary – it may just take adding a little extra effort, extra attention to detail or extra care, to one of them, in order to turn it into something extra-ordinary. This applies to service too. Extra-ordinary or 5-Star service providers are willing to do the little extra things which ordinary service providers are not willing to do. The ordinary choose to remain in their comfort zone and their usual way of doing things, so they find excuses for not going the extra-mile.

"We provide free shipping and free return shipping...for all of our customers as a standard part of our service. And although we promise our customers they will receive their shoes within 4-5 days, we upgrade the service for almost all of our customers...It's not something we have to do, and it's not something that will increase our profits in

the short term. But because it's something that creates a great customer experience, we choose to do it, because we believe that in the long run, little things that keep the customer in mind will end up paying huge dividends."
- TONY HSIEH | CEO, ZAPPOS.COM

When I ordered proof copies of my book, *"Making Success Deliberate – How to Develop and Sustain a Personal Effectiveness & Leadership Excellence Brand,"* I expected delivery not less than 4 weeks later. CreateSpace, an Amazon.com company, delivered from the USA to Africa in less than 7 days. This exceeded my expectations, especially comparing with previous experiences with other Print-On-Demand service providers.

Service in the "no-hair" business

Whatever your craft is, how you serve your customers will determine the growth or limitation of your business. As long as you have a single person who depends on your service to meet one or more of their needs, it means you are in the service business – you are a service provider and those you serve deserve and expect superior service from you.

My personal barber has taken hospitality quite seriously. Popularly known as *"Devah"* or *"Moyo,"* Davison Musiringi has enjoyed success in his line of work for more than two decades, on the basis of service excellence and a focused relationship management strategy. A lot of companies and professionals could learn quite a lot from this dedicated barber.

He has good communication skills, respectful, smart and hygienic, always putting on a necktie, to mirror his chosen target market. He schedules his clients appropriately, sending reminders by sms or calling, even offers home visits and service on credit where necessary. By so doing, this responsive barber has managed to define his market niche and serves the managers and business people within the city – his relationship management skills extends his reach to their other family members as well. I have seen him on countless times servicing his machines to ensure they are as friendly as possible, to the smooth skin of his important clients. He runs his work like a well-oiled machine in order to please all his customers. This is a barber who goes beyond the ordinary.

You might be in a field that seems very common to all and easy to be taken for granted by both service providers and customers. 5-Star Customer Service is required in all market segments. Zappos.com has done it in online selling of shoes and other personal accessories, Multichoice in satellite television services, ExtraC-

5-Star Customer Service

ity Luxury in passenger transportation and Avenues Clinic in medical care. You can also make a 5-Star difference in your peculiar area of specialty.

LEARNING QUESTIONS

1. In your line of business or profession, how can you do those ordinary things or provide those ordinary products in an extra-ordinary way?

2. Can you identify and list the opportunities to grow your business based on improved customer service?

3. You might not be a global business, but how can you transform your service to World-Class standards?

F) DO IT RIGHT THE FIRST TIME AND ALL THE TIME

Efficient Seamless Service (ESS) must be part of a 5-Star Customer Service brand. This means consistent service quality - *wherever you go, whenever you go and whoever you deal with.*

The exceptional *"refreshing"* greeting at Rainbow Tourism Group (RTG) Hotels, from the cleaner, to waitress and even directors, is a fitting example of seamless service associated

5-Star Customer Service

with a brand. This was noticed by two of our visitors on a nation-wide business tour. They admitted they had forgotten a lot of things about the hotels and their appearances, but they were still impressed by the consistent and refreshing standard in the way they were greeted at every RTG hotel they visited.

Consistency and Efficiency are required in both customer care issues and customer service delivery.

"47% of customers say contacting a company multiple times for the same issue is the most frustrating aspect of poor customer service."
- STATE OF MULTICHANNEL CUSTOMER SERVICE SURVEY

LEARNING QUESTIONS

1. Service quality at start of day and at end of day/shift must be consistent – how consistent are you, how much is your attitude charged? Can it last the whole shift/day?

2. How can you ensure you remain enthused throughout the day?

3. Do you offer same service quality and attitude to *"high-value"* customers and *"low-value"* customers? What enables you to consistently do this, whilst customising the service to their unique needs and expectations?

4. How consistent is your service quality across branches, business units or at different times?

G) REMEMBER - IT'S NOT ABOUT YOU, IT'S ABOUT THE CUSTOMER

Service providers take lightly, the basic marketing principle of starting with the needs of the customer in mind, yet this remains the core element and foundation of 5-Star Customer Service. You can never deliver excellent service without a thorough understanding of the needs of your customers. The principle of empathy is critical in this process, i.e. trying to put yourself in the other person's shoes as you *"do for others what you would want to be done for you"* if you went somewhere else requesting a service or product.

As a service provider, when you begin to think in this manner, it becomes easier and more instinctive to appreciate and consider the needs of those you serve in all situations. In his book, *"The Seven Habits of Highly Effective People,"* the late Stephen Covey put this well in Habit 5, when he states – *"Seek first to understand, and then to be understood."*

Aim to provide 5-Star Customer Service:

1. Seek first to understand what the needs of your customers are. You must ask yourself, *"How would my customers define excellent service. What does it mean to them?"* You process thoughts like: *"If I was the person on the other side of the counter, how would I want to be treated?"*

2. When you make decisions, you don't focus on what makes life easier for you, in isolation to the impact of the decision on your customers. Always have the customer in mind – others call it, being *"customer-focused"* all the time.

3. The customer defines what excellent service is, not the service provider. Just like *'beauty lies in the eye of the beholder'* – excellent service lies in the heart, ear, eye, taste, smell and feeling of the customer.

LEARNING STORY – IT'S ABOUT WHAT THE CUSTOMER EXPECTS

Some time ago, one of our companies got a job to re-do sub-standard work that had been done by another service provider. It was a car park shade for a leading parastatal. We fitted a very expensive and the most durable material available, but in a slightly different shade to the one they wanted. The technical specifications confirming the quality and strength of material used did not matter, as we could not convince the client to keep that shade.

They were so much unimpressed that they even pointed to any signs of stretch-marks, as reasons for their rejection. We went ahead to remove the more expensive material and bought the one that appealed to their corporate brand, at a cost lower to us by more than one third, but a quality cheaper than the original material. After this adjustment, we had ourselves a very happy customer.

At the end of it all, it was not about what we thought was best or what we wanted. It was about what the customer thought was best for them. The definition of quality and excellent service was theirs to make. All we could do was offer our technical advice, to help make their decision more informed, especially with regards to quality and durability of the material they chose.

LEARNING STORY – "MY NAME IS…"

During one of my training sessions with branch staff from a major commercial bank, a customer service officer shared a story about a *"Comrade"* who taught her this customer service principle.

5-Star Customer Service

The customer happened to be a well-known politician at that time. She had come in response to a call advising that her cheque book was ready for collection. On receiving the cheque book and signing for it, she flipped through the pages, only moments later, to frown and toss it back onto the counter. She went on to demand, *"This is not my cheque book, please take it back and advise when mine is ready for collection."*

Looking a bit confused, the customer service officer picked the cheque book, convinced that it belonged to the customer, opened the pages and politely asserted, *"I am not sure if there is some kind of misunderstanding, but the cheque book has your name on it and I am certain it should belong to you, unless there are some errors you have picked."*

She never expected the response that was to come, but it made her totally agree with the point we were discussing in that training session – that customers have their own thoughts and feelings about what excellent service is all about. The customer's response was simple, *"If you are to check on the request form I submitted ordering the cheque book, you will find that the name to be printed on my cheque book was put as 'Cde (for Comrade).....' and this cheque book has been printed for 'Mrs ....'"*

It is not about how we want to refer to people, it's about how they want their names and titles to be used, which makes it excellent service, or bad service, to them. If they are a *Professor*, please don't refer to them as "*Doctor*" – the least you can do is to respect the fact that they earned their title.

H) ENSURE CONVENIENCE & ACCESSIBILITY

Convenience should not be crafted, primarily, with the service provider in mind. The customer must come first. Years ago, banks in Zimbabwe and other parts of the world would work half the day on Wednesdays. This would enable bank staff and officials to have an afternoon of golf, other sporting events and games, besides balancing regulated working hours. The unfortunate thing was that no consideration was given to customer needs. Customers had to take it as it was and were forced to plan around the official banking hours gazetted by the regulations.

As banking systems and regulations continue to evolve, we will continue to see more opportunities for 24-hour accessibility, including longer banking hours extended for the convenience of customers. In Zimbabwe, banks like CBZ and BancABC, and in Uganda and South Africa, a branch of Barclays bank and ABSA bank, respectively, have already taken the lead in this regard. Supermarkets are following suit and some fuel stations have returned to the 24-hour service practice they had stopped.

Accessibility, on another focus-area, means the availability of key personnel to adequately address concerns raised by customers. The lack of two-way communication mechanisms leads to increased frustration of customers as well as negative staff attitudes as staff know there are sufficient gatekeepers protecting the management ears from the *"noise"* coming from customer complaints. This, in turn, makes dissatisfied customers walk across to the competition without giving the organisation a chance to address issues of concern.

LEARNING QUESTIONS

1. In what ways are you seeking to increase the convenience you extend to customers? What have you done in the past 12 months?

2. How open is the door, for customers to directly access your management, whether in person, by phone or via email?

I) LEVERAGE TECHNOLOGY

Advancements towards solutions that are internet-based and mobile telecommunications-based are supposed to be utilized by service providers to enhance the quality of service, especially for extending convenience and reduction of costs/prices.

For customers who are allergic to queues, like I am, excellent service can be easily derived from user-friendly service technologies like automated switch boards, **user-friendly** internet banking, smart ATMs, POS access points, effective and reliable mobile banking platforms like Ecocash. Other examples include employee intranet facilities, online application forms, online training/tuition and mobile/online tracking of parcels or vehicles.

Multichoice Africa and Econet are great examples of service providers who have managed to use a combination of tech-based solutions to extend convenience, respond to and reduce customer complaints about delays in service.

Multichoice Africa's DSTV subscribers used to have nightmares trying to get queries resolved, service restored or activated, make payments or switch between packages. Back then you had to make phone calls every other month or visit the service office often and join the long

5-Star Customer Service

queues. Now it's been years since I spoke to anyone at Multichoice, because of the way they have employed technology to address almost every complaint that customers used to raise.

You can now clear any *'signal-scrambling'* error via your cell phone or the internet, if their in-built and pre-scheduled automated clearing system fails to pick your unique case. You can pay via Ecocash mobile banking (and many other payment channels), from the comfort of your own home, including shifting between packages, depending on what you can afford at any given time.

Econet has made it easier for customers to make phone calls, browse the internet, effect various financial transactions including paying utility bills, online payments, saving, access insurance cover, connect or track vehicles and network on social media platforms – all interfaced on the same mobile phone platform. The Ecocash platform has been instrumental in empowering other service providers to extend this convenience to their own customers.

This is the empowerment and convenience, which technology is supposed to extend to the customer. You can contrast this with other service providers who remain rigid and unresponsive to both customer needs and technological advancement. If they fail to respond in good time, their place will be guaranteed in the corporate museum.

LEARNING QUESTIONS

1. Can you think of different ways, through which you can empower your customers and extend unparalleled convenience by employing different technologies applicable to your line of business?

2. Identify and list some of the benefits of leveraging technology, to both your customers and your business?

The slow uptake of technology by service providers will remain one of the reasons why there will always be opportunities for innovative and responsive players in most markets.

More will need to be done, as there remains a few challenges hampering the effective use of technology to improve the quality of customer service, especially in Africa and other emerging markets.

These include:

♦ Lack of innovation and limited tech-skills.

- Slow uptake of technology by customers due to cultural influences and the comfort zone created by old technologies.

- Affordability challenges due to lack of resources required by customers to acquire devices compatible with tech-based service solutions.

- Access limited to those who can afford or in areas with connectivity.

- Economies not ready due to unavailability of adequate infrastructure.

Africa must realise she has no option - this is the present and future reality. The world is connected through, and riding on, technology. No more questions of readiness, we must get on board or become extinct! The world has become a connected global village and there are no special favours or affirmative action for the slow or the rigid.

J) MAINTAIN PRIVACY & CONFIDENTIALITY

A senior nursing sister who attended one of our workshops, shared a story that I will never forget. She said this actually happened decades ago whilst she was still a trainee.

She described how one of the nurses walked out of a clinic with an elderly man following closely behind her. There were a couple of growing queues outside, as patients waited for treatment early in the morning. The nurse shouted, as she sought the attention of everyone present, *"Can someone tell this gentlemen what I said earlier. I thought I made it very clear that, the first queue is for mothers with children, the second for those who require change of dressing and the third one over there, for people with sexually transmitted infections. Sir, please join the third queue!"*

LEARNING QUESTIONS

1. How are you building your customers' trust and confidence in your service? What are you doing to protect their private and confidential information?

2. How secure are your manual and electronic systems?

3. In what ways can your department or organisation improve the respect extended to the dignity of customers?

"Businesses and users are going to use technology only if they can trust it."
SATYA NADELLA - CEO, MICROSOFT

K) REMAIN RELEVANT – ADD VALUE

How you put all these tools to use will determine whether you will remain relevant to your customers or not.

How will you start adding value to your customers so you can remain relevant in meeting their needs?

- Satisfy your customers by delivering what you promise.

- Resolve their complaints effectively.

- Effectively listen to them and be responsive to their dynamic needs.

- Seek to understand and address the issues which affect them the most.

- **Predict The Future Needs of Your Customers**

Chapter 8

EFFECTIVE COMMUNICATION

"The question isn't, 'What do we want to know about people?' it's, 'What do people want to tell about themselves?'"
–MARK ZUCKERBERG | CEO, FACEBOOK

INTERPERSONAL COMMUNICATION

♦ Communication is the bedrock and the centre of excellent customer service.

Effective Communication

Effective communication takes place when the receiver of the message gets the same idea that the sender had when she sent the message. The element of consensus of the minds or getting the same picture about the message exchanged, makes communication effective. Two people can exchange words, but as long as they end up with two different impressions of the same words – effective communication has not taken place.

Two-way Communication

The need for feedback between communicating parties helps to clarify any misunderstandings and enables consensus or *meeting of the minds*. 5-Star service providers must always promote two-way communication. This enables them to get the same picture that a customer has in their mind when making a service request. This facilitates responsive action better suited to meet or exceed the customer's expectation.

Communication barriers

Most of the time, communication ends up being ineffective or distorted due to the existence of barriers to effective communication. These barriers need to be eliminated or managed effectively. They include:

i. **Jargon**
    Every line of business has a language peculiar to it. Service providers must be careful to always adjust their language accordingly, whenever dealing with those outside their areas of specialty.

    As a service provider to those I train, I find myself reading medical journals, car magazines, local governance resources, humanitarian reports, financial news, technology articles and political news. Sometimes, I conduct in-depth research so that my examples, choice of words and case study exercises become relevant to my target participants. Even in medical school, there is a course to help students communicate medical issues using simplified *everyday language*.

ii. **Differences in language & culture**
Sign language, drawings, diagrams or maps can help deal with the language barrier. Service providers can go beyond the expected and learn a new language or appreciate different cultures so as to effectively deal with customers from different communities and nationalities.

iii. **Prejudice**
We are all prejudiced! Each one of us has their own preferences, things we like and others we don't like, based on our personal beliefs, cultural background, values and attitude. This makes it imperative for service providers to adopt an open-mind when dealing with customers. It is the challenge for every service provider to develop their Emotional Intelligence, as advocated for, under **Star 3** – *"Attitude and The Personal Brand."*

iv. **Age and Generation gap**
The dynamics of time and culture progression always usher-in differences in exposure, perceptions and values, between different generations. Understanding and adjusting to this reality will enable service providers to please customers from different age groups and generations.

v. **Channel & Mode of communication**
Service providers must always define their target customers and the intended effect of any communication they make. This will assist in selecting the most effective channel and the appropriate mode of communication. Even in our families, it is not everyone who has the tact to break sad news to relatives and friends.

vi. **Distance**
Distance can include the question of whether to shout or whisper, to use the phone or send a person. It can also mean being careful not to be too close or too far, in a way that makes customers uncomfortable.

vii. **Noise & other distractions**
Noise can be physical or psychological. The noise of a passing truck or a power generator can be as distracting as the noise in the mind of a person who is thinking about how

slowly time is moving as they look forward to taking their lunch break.

LEARNING QUESTIONS

1. In you line of work, which barriers to communication do you deal with the most? How have you managed to reduce or eliminate their impact on the effectiveness of your communication with customers?

2. With the help of your team mates, can you identify your own prejudices and find ways to guard against them?

VERBAL COMMUNICATION

Verbal communication consists of the choice of words and language used by the speaker and the listener. It makes up the content of the message, determining whether it has been *"pitched"* at the right level for the listener to understand.

a) Choice of a language understandable by both parties is most ideal – otherwise the use of drawings, an interpreter or translator becomes necessary.

b) Choice of words – avoiding jargon, verbosity, *vaguity* and ambiguity. The purpose of effective communication is to provide service on the basis of mutual understanding, not to *'impress'* customers with *'big'* words.

LEARNING STORY

Years ago, as I watched the news on TV, I felt pity for some primary school children at a rural school. Two senior politicians had descended on their school to hand over some donations. Whilst I had no problems with them addressing school children in English, my concern became the level of vocabulary at which they chose to pitch their speeches. I had to look up some of the words from my dictionary. I was left wondering if effective communication had taken place.

♦ Are you using your words and language effectively and intentionally, to derive desired results from your communication efforts?

VOCAL COMMUNICATION

Vocal communication is the manipulation of your vocal codes to communicate through the sound of your voice. This includes examples like whistling, singing, laughing, screaming or sighing, among others. Vocal communication skills determine how the message is said and will influence how it will be interpreted by the listener.

Be careful not to become like my *"brothers in the neighbourhood."* You must have met some of them by now. They always speak the *"queen's language"* with exaggerated intonation, forcing most of their English to escape through the nose. The irony is that, after every other statement they mutter, they have the audacity to ask, *"You-know-what-I'm-saying!"* My usual response is that, *"I don't know what you are saying, and will not know until you start speaking clearly!"*

♦ Learn to speak clearly and audibly.

CONVERSATION SKILLS

Develop your conversation skills so that you can communicate effectively and please your customers. Conversations are important because they enable service providers to understand their customers and their needs better. They are also a foundational platform on which relationships are built.

a) Welcome and Greeting
RTG's *"refreshing morning"* greeting, is an example of service providers taking time and effort to make the way they welcome and greet people *"a unique memorable experience."* How are you making your customers

feel welcome and special whenever they come to your workplace?

b) **Asking the right Questions**
Whether it is attending to a breakdown of equipment underground, conducting a prognosis on a medical patient or determining the source of a complaint in a bank; asking the right questions is the essential element required to quickly get you to provide solutions that will satisfy your customers.

It is always useful to know:

- **When to use open questions.**
Remember the 5Ws and 1H? These begin with *"Why," "When," "Where," "What," "Who"* and *"How."* These questions will help, if you want to draw as much information from customers as possible. They help you to better understand customers and their needs because they allow the customer to explain and give elaborate detail.
- **When to use closed questions**
Closed questions can be used to guide customers as you seek to draw specific information. They become quite useful in emergency situations and when you need to summarise and bring a long, winding conversation to a conclusion. (They are the real *'conversation-killers.'*) This means, you must avoid closed questions when you want to

draw information and find out as much as you can, from your customer.

c) Proper use of names and titles

> *"Employees only ask for the customer's name 21% of the time."*
> -CONTACTPOINT CLIENT RESEARCH

Using a customer's name personalises the service experience. It gives the customer a sense of belonging and the comforting feeling that they are not dealing with a stranger. It can be rude or offending to customers if service providers do not use their names in the way they prefer. Remember the Learning Story about the *"Comrade"* and her cheque book?

d) Listening more than you speak

Show interest in the customer and what they say, more than your eagerness to tell them what you know. The best counsellors and the best sales people are found amongst the world's best listeners, not just speakers. It is listening well, that will enable you to offer relevant solutions because you would have determined exactly what customers expect from you.

When you ask questions, your top priority must be to listen effectively so that you can offer the relevant response.

e) Closing a Conversation or Customer encounter

Summarise your conversation, confirm issues agreed upon, verify and clarify any sticking points, thank the customer for trusting you to serve them, wish them well and extend an open door to assist them again.

THE IMPORTANCE OF POSITIVE BODY LANGUAGE

Action speaks louder than words, so strive to keep your word, every time. If something gets in the way of you fulfilling your promise, communicate proactively. Don't wait for customers to complain before you can take action.

a) Image & Personal Hygiene
- Dress appropriately for each occasion.
- Make sure you make others feel comfortable being around you – bath, brush your teeth, use a deodorant, wear fresh and clean clothes.
- Let your image give a good impression every time.

b) The First Impression
- There is only one chance to make a first impression. If you lose it, you may never get another opportunity to make amends.

- Do it right the first time, all the time – always be ready to make a good first impression.
- Manage you appearance, confidence level, environment around you, your posture, the sound/tone of your voice and the first words you say. All these will influence the quality of the first impressions you generate.

c) The Last Impression
- The last impression is equally as important as the first impression.
- A firm handshake, thanking the customer, availing contact details, extending an open door for future assistance and wishing the customer well – are all important elements of making a great last impression.
- Above all, do what you promise the customer.

SHOW ME YOU CARE – DON'T TELL ME!

Don't wait for my complaint.
Confirm you care, through your body language.
Your facial expression, when you welcome me or when I approach you for service just before your lunch break, says a lot. Don't speak to me and tell me you care – let me look at you and see how much you care, let my experience of your service make me know that you genuinely care.
Show me you care.

Communication as a Tool for Enhancing Customer Loyalty

A major financial institution lost a significant amount of customers' money as a result of a fraud. It ended up with its forex trading license withdrawn by the authorities. The bank communicated to its clients all the efforts it was making to refund the lost money and the clients remained loyal and supportive. A few years later, an unrelated insurer faced liquidity challenges and could not settle its customers' claims. The insurers' staff and senior management were dodgy, never communicated and ignored clients' correspondences and clients responded by taking legal action and taking their business elsewhere.

The insurer's license was revoked and it was forced to close its business. The bank managed to retain its customers, repay lost funds, got its forex license restored and continues to grow as a business.

LISTENING SKILLS

82% of people would rather talk to a good listener than to a good speaker.

"Two elderly ladies were sitting on their porch one summer evening, enjoying the warm breeze. The crickets were awake in the field, and their music competed only with that of the church choir down the road, which was practicing for Sunday morning. One of the women, who was enraptured by the choir's singing, commented dreamily, 'Isn't that a beautiful sound?' The other woman, who rocked gently in time to the sounds of the crickets, replied, 'Oh, yes. I understand they do it by rubbing their hind legs together.'" — UNKNOWN

- Customers will know you listen well, only when you respond in a way that addresses their needs and requests.

- You will listen effectively if you adopt an open mind and manage your prejudices.

- Asking follow-up questions to clarify what a customer has said is a sign of good listening skills.

LEARNING STORY – WHO DO YOU LISTEN TO?[3]

In a much publicised story, a three and a half year old Sainsbury's customer, got help from her mother to write the British supermarket chain about how their *"tiger bread"* looked more like a giraffe.

Sainsbury's Customer Support Manager, went on to respond to the letter in writing, explaining how the bread got its name, *"I think renaming tiger bread giraffe bread is a brilliant idea - it looks much more like the blotches on a giraffe than the stripes on a tiger, doesn't it? It is called tiger bread because the first baker who made it a loooong time ago thought it looked stripey like a tiger. Maybe they were a bit silly."* The manager went on to send the young customer a gift card for some shopping experience.

Sainsbury did what is expected of a 5-Star Customer Service provider, and went on to change the name of the bread to *"giraffe bread."* They announced the change posting notices in their supermarkets reading, *"Thanks to a clever suggestion from one of our customers, we've changed the name of our tiger bread to giraffe bread. Don't worry, the recipe hasn't changed and the bread still tastes as great as ever."*

Compare this to my experience with the bus company in the first Learning Story of this book!

LEARNING QUESTIONS

1. What is the Importance of Effective Listening to your Customer Service quality?

2. How well are you demonstrating good listening skills in responding to the service delivery and support requests made by your customers?

3. How do you determine whether you have listened effectively or not?

4. What stops you from listening to ALL your customers? How can you guard against such an attitude?

5-Star Customer Service

Chapter 9

COMMUNICATION TECHNOLOGIES

"By 2020, it is anticipated there will be more than 50 billion connected devices globally, with mobile being the primary internet device for most individuals... The challenge is how to transition from existing product and traditional distribution models to those that deliver what customers want."
−ERNST & YOUNG

EFFECTIVE USE OF THE TELEPHONE

During a workshop for a financial institution, a gentlemen shared the story of how he got his job at the newly opened bank. The way he answered the telephone and professionally handled conversations with clients for his previous employer, made the CEO of the new bank to assign his HR Director to *"get the gentlemen operating their switchboard at all cost."*

- How professional are you in answering the telephone and handling conversations with customers?
- What is your standard for answering the phone?

International Best Practice

1. The phone should not ring for more than 3 times before it is answered.

2. You must first greet the customer, with appreciation.

3. Identify your organisation. If you are answering from an extension, just identify your department or section. You do not need to repeat the name of the organisation as this would have been done at the switchboard.

4. Introduce yourself so that the customer knows who they are speaking with. Most of the time, this prompts the customer to give you their own name without you having to ask them. It also gives them confidence as it confirms ownership of your part of the conversation. If the call gets disconnected, the customer can conveniently ask for you by name, instead of being transferred from person to person, trying to find out who they were speaking with.

5. Politely ask how you may help. This enables you to take charge of the conversation – the person who asks questions is normally the one in charge.

5-Star examples of how to answer the telephone:

♦ *"Thank you for calling 5-Star Services, this is Archibald, how may I help you?"*

♦ *"Good afternoon, 5-Star Services, this is Archibald, how may I serve you?"*

Important tips on Telephone Skills

a) Ask for their preference, before putting them on hold. If it will take time, ask if you can call them back or if they want to call back.

b) Whenever you promise to call back – please do so within the agreed timeframe.

c) When referring and transferring a call to another person, make sure the customer does not get to repeat their request. Always give a summary of the story before putting the customer through. Also ensure the person in the other office is available, avoid transferring and putting your phone down before someone answers the call.

"A majority of 63% of customers still believes that the phone provides the highest level of customer service"
-ACCENT MARKETING

"On a global scale, 92% of customers still prefer phone and talking to a live person."

WEBSITES AND EMAIL COMMUNICATION

Most websites are nothing more than the internet version of a static bill board or poster. There must be much more to your online strategy than mere web-presence. Gain appreciation of Search Engine Optimisation (SEO) and other analytic tools. Research and get training on how to adopt an effective online presence to better serve your customers and derive value for your business.

"89% of customers have stopped shopping at online stores after experiencing poor customer service."
- MERLIN

"41% of customers expect an email response within 6 hours."
- FORRESTER RESEARCH INC.

51% of customers did not receive a response after sending an email inquiry/report."
-BENCHMARK PORTAL

- Always respond to emails timely, if possible within 24 hours – even if it means just to acknowledge receipt and giving an indication of when you can give a more relevant response.

- Never put email addresses on your website and business card, when you know that no one will check or respond to emails sent to those addresses.

CALL CENTRES AND ANSWERING MACHINES

"67% of customers have hung up the phone out of frustration they could not talk to a real person"
 -AMERICAN EXPRESS SURVEY

"75% of customers believe it takes too long to reach a live agent"
 - HARRIS INTERACTIVE

Putting in place a service and support call centre has a number of benefits, including:

1. 24-hour accessibility of customer service and support functions.
2. Provision of the *"personal/human touch"* when attending to customer needs.
3. Platform for identification of new customer needs, common problems and complaints.
4. Opportunity to cross-sell and up-sell the company's products and services.

The Personal touch

- Learn from the progress and difference being made in Customer Service, by call centres at Econet, Bulawayo City Council, Steward Bank and Multichoice.

- Take ownership of your customers' experiences and, wherever possible, avoid outsourcing call centre functions.

MOBILE DEVICES

The Future Is Already Here!

"By 2020, it is anticipated there will be more than 50 billion connected devices globally, with mobile being the primary internet device for most individuals... The challenge is how to transition from existing product and traditional distribution models to those that deliver what customers want."
ERNST & YOUNG

"By 2016, 50% of all retail dollars spent in the US will be influenced digitally... 87% of the world now owns mobile phones and 1.2 billion use their devices to access the internet"
- IBM DIGITAL CUSTOMER EXPERIENCE REPORT

'We're seeing things move away from auto-centric societies to mobility-centric societies.'
RACHEL NGUYEN DIRECTOR, GLOBAL UPSTREAM PLANNING, NISSAN MOTOR CO., LTD.

SOCIAL MEDIA PLATFORMS

"52% say Facebook is the most effective social channel for customer service with Twitter following at 25%."
THE SOCIAL CUSTOMER ENGAGEMENT INDEX

"45% of companies offering web and mobile self-service reported an increase in site traffic and reduced phone enquiries."
- CRM MAGAZINE

"Over 1 million people view tweets about customer service every week. Roughly 80% of those are negative or critical in nature."
- TOUCH AGENCY

"Customers who engage with companies over social media spend 20% to 40% more money with those companies than other customers."
- BAIN & COMPANY

LEARNING QUESTIONS

1. What new ways can you come up with, to offer memorable experiences to your customers through the use of Communication Technologies?

2. How can you use the statistics given above, to reflect on your own customer service and interaction strategies, to improve your level of service?

3. What is your social media or online strategy for enhancing customer experiences?

4. How much of your products and services, can be accessed via the internet? What can you do, to improve this?

Chapter 10

ATTITUDE & THE PERSONAL BRAND

"Excellence is not a skill. It's an Attitude.
–UNKNOWN

THE IMPORTANCE OF A POSITIVE ATTITUDE

"45% of customers say a friendly customer service representative is one of the top components of excellent customer service"
- MERLIN

Whilst your attitude as a service provider is very important, you must realise that no one else can change that attitude. The door to your attitude is locked from inside and the only key to access it, is in your hand. Your attitude is your personal responsibility, no one else can change it for you. Whatever is done from the outside and by others, is just knocking – the decision to open the door is solely each individual's.

- You cannot separate service from the person offering it – service is an art.

- In Customer Service – When the going gets tough, *a Positive Attitude keeps you going*. It is the power that fuels enthusiasm.

- Attitude is your mind-set, it is what makes you do what you do in the way you do it, what makes you respond to customers the way you do. It is the *"spirit"* behind your actions – *the flavour of your customer service*.

- There is so much knowledge and skill, yet little practice of the knowledge and skills. Most of the times, the bridge needed to close the gap between knowledge and performance is the attitude-factor.

WHAT WILL HELP YOU ADOPT A POSITIVE ATTITUDE?

The tools to help you change your attitude for the better are thoroughly covered in two of my books, *"I Want To Change – Becoming A Better You"* and *"It's My Life – Taking Personal Responsibility for Your Destiny."* Below I summarise a few focus areas covered in these books, to help you adopt a positive attitude:

5-Star Customer Service

1. Love what you do and love the people you do it for.
2. Always think of your Customers.
3. Fully develop your intrapersonal skills.
4. Reprogram the underlying elements which influence your behaviour and habits.

LEARNING STORY

On more than one occasion, I have been asked by colleagues, *"Why do you work like this is your father's company. Why are you doing this to yourself?"*

An example is when I had to stand by the roadside hiking, with my bags and training equipment, traveling some 300km to conduct training for one of my former employers, who happened to be a listed financial institution.

These weekend trainings had no overtime payment. The administration department would refuse to release a vehicle and I would escalate the issue to my immediate manager, who was the HR Director. Her response: *"Archie if these guys won't give you the tools, go home and play with your kids. No one will fire you for that!"*

Appreciating that I already had participants traveling from other parts of the country to the training venue, I would find myself by the roadside, with all my bags and training equipment, hiking on a Saturday morning in order to start training as soon as the bank closed for the day. The training would run until 10pm on a Saturday, then from 8am until lunch time on the Sunday and I would be back in the office on Monday morning.

What made me do things, the way I did them?

a) I loved what I was doing. No one was holding a gun to my head to wake up in the morning and spend the whole day facilitating training sessions.

b) I never saw myself as an employee. I was not working for the bank, I was working for myself. I was an *"intrapreneur"* who saw himself as a partner to the bank because it availed the platform for me to practice and develop my skill and be able to shine as a personal brand.

c) I had respect for the people who were depending on me for their personal and professional development.

d) I decided a long time ago, that I will not live a life of excuses or become a victim who is always looking for sympathy.

e) I always cherish the opportunity to do the little extra things that ordinary people will refuse to do! I want to be Extraordinary.

f) The reason why all the statements above begin with "I" is that, adopting such a mind-set is a personal responsibility/decision. I did not have to do what I did – I chose to.

> *"The quality of an individual is reflected in the standards they set for themselves."*
> -RAY CROC

LEARNING QUESTIONS

1. What makes you do what you do, in the way you do it?

2. Considering your current circumstances, what attitude do you choose to adopt. What mind-set will enable you to be enthusiastic about life, your job and your customers?

3. Besides the contractual remuneration, what opportunities do you see your organisation giving you for personal brand development and how can you begin to utilise the opportunities to shine?

4. Evaluate the kind of attitude to which, you and your colleagues expose your internal and external customers. List the areas you need to change and examples of ways in which you can begin to make positive adjustments.

INTRAPERSONAL COMMUNICATION

Improving you attitude means developing your intrapersonal communication processes. The two books mentioned earlier in this chapter, as well as *"Making Success Deliberate – How to Develop and Sustain a Personal Effectiveness & Leadership Excellence Brand"* are referral texts on the different strategies and tools to enhance your intrapersonal skills and to help you build a personal brand of effectiveness and excellence.

1. The Motivation Value Chain covered in *"Making Success Deliberate"* helps you to sustain change, of both attitude and behaviour, on the basis of understanding how they are influenced by your personal values, beliefs and the mapping of your mind.

2. The in-depth research on how you can use your mind as a faithful servant to help you take charge of your own life, is covered in *"I Want To Change – Becoming A Better You"* and *"It's My Life – Taking Personal Responsibility for Your Destiny."*

3. The following summary of Emotional Intelligence qualities from the book *"Primal Leadership – Realising the Power of Emotional Intelligence" by Daniel Goleman with Richard Boyatzis and Annie McKee*, is a guiding resource and reference for your personal development

strategy covering both your intrapersonal and interpersonal skills[8]:

Self-awareness

- *Emotional self-awareness:* Reading one's own emotions and recognizing their impact and using "gut sense" to guide decisions.
- *Accurate self-assessment:* Knowing one's strengths and limits.
- *Self-confidence:* A sound sense of one's self-worth and capabilities.

Self-management

- *Emotional self-control:* Keeping disruptive emotions and impulses under control.
- *Transparency:* Displaying honesty, integrity and trustworthiness.
- *Adaptability:* Flexibility in adapting to changing situations or overcoming obstacles.
- *Achievement:* The drive to improve performance to meet inner standards of excellence.
- *Initiative:* Readiness to act and seize opportunities.
- *Optimism:* Seeing the upside in events.

Social Awareness

- *Empathy:* Sensing others' emotions, understanding their perspective, and taking active interest in their concerns.
- *Organizational awareness:* Reading the currents, decision networks, and politics at the organizational level.
- *Service:* Recognizing and meeting follower, client or customer needs.

Relationship Management

- *Inspirational leadership:* Guiding and motivating with a compelling vision.
- *Influence:* Wielding a range of tactics for persuasion.
- *Developing others:* Bolstering others' abilities through feedback and guidance.
- *Change catalyst:* Initiating, managing and leading in new directions.
- *Building bonds:* Cultivating and maintaining relationship webs.
- *Teamwork and collaboration:* Cooperation and team-building.

PERSONAL DEVELOPMENT

"One important key to success is self-confidence. An important key to self-confidence is preparation"
- ARTHUR ASHE

When you invest in your personal development, you are preparing yourself for success as a 5-Star Customer service provider.

1. **Training & Personal Improvement**
   Attend training programs and enrol for certification and qualifications relevant for the progression of your personal development plan.

2. **Specialised Study and Research**
   Go beyond general knowledge and seek to become an expert and authentic voice in your area of specialty.

3. **Practicing**
Translate acquired knowledge and skills into practice. Aim for performance excellence as you attain Practitioner-status.

Personal Effectiveness & Leadership Excellence (P.E.L.E)

In the Personal Development book, *"Making Success Deliberate – How to Develop and Sustain a Personal Effectiveness & Leadership Excellence Brand,"* I cover in detail, the need to be effective and successful. To help you enhance your personal brand as a 5-Star Customer Service provider, a summary of what the three book sections offer, is given below:

1. *Know and Master yourself* – Define yourself, what is your mission on earth, how do you see yourself fulfilling that mission? What are the beliefs that give life, spirit and passion to your dream and which values will guide your decisions and actions for you to be fulfilled by your own success. How will you make sure all these things are aligned so that they translate into the kind of personal brand you want to present to the world? These elements will help you adopt the personal discipline required to focus your decisions and efforts for success. You must have a clear personal philosophy about what success means to you.

2. ***Execute your personal Strategy*** – Have a clear plan or strategy to translate your success philosophy into desired results. Adopt a productive work ethic, with a laser-focus and requisite execution strategies to produce results. Don't waste time and avoid the company of wasteful people who lack the desire to achieve. Become assertive and action-oriented. Directly or indirectly recruit a team of people who will enable you to produce results. Everywhere you look around, production must be taking place to bring you closer to realizing your personal definition of success. You must adopt a personal responsibility strategy to enable the realization of your dreams.

3. *Craft a lasting Legacy* – Do not seek success just for the sake of succeeding or for self-gratification. Seek a life of impact and significance. Plan the sustainability of your success so that you do not drift back to failure and mediocrity. Do not plan to die, do not plan for the death of your name or influence - rather, plan for the resting of a life well lived. Plan who will be the rightful people to perpetuate your success story, how you want to be remembered, how you can continue to inspire other generations towards success. Whilst you still live, how do you begin to share your success with others – I have realized there is more fulfilment when sharing with others than enjoying on my own,

whatever success achieved. Craft a plan to remain alive even after you are dead and long gone.

> *"Whatever you vividly imagine, ardently desire, sincerely believe and enthusiastically act upon – must inevitably come to pass."*
> - PAUL J. MEYER

LEARNING STORY - COMPLAINTS CONVERSION

Making a Difference through a Positive Attitude

With a positive attitude, you can learn how to convert complaints into platforms for creating loyal customers. During the hyperinflationary economic environment in Zimbabwe, I was a Retail Banking Branch manager. I had an irate customer walk into my office one day. She was fuming because (as she put it), *"your staff down stairs are giving their friends and relatives cash whilst those of us without friends in this bank, are told to wait or come back the following day."*

After listening to her complaint and frustration, we came to the understanding that the nature of her organisation's business actually warranted that we facilitate that their employees get a special arrangement for their cash requirements. We ended up agreeing on a pre-order system, enabling all of them to come as soon as their ordered cash requirement became available. This worked out well and led to a few more new accounts opened from the same humanitarian organisation.

When you are daily pressed with demands and complaints like the one above, it will take a positive attitude to remain calm, help the customer calm down and begin to objectively look at ways you can resolve the complaint to the customer's satisfaction. Almost a decade later, we remain good friends with the once irate customer and she still banks with my former employer.

THE COST OF A NEGATIVE ATTITUDE

At the beginning of Chapter 2, I related the story of the negative attitude displayed by staff of a contractor engaged by a big mining house. The incident caused by this indifference, cost a number of employees their jobs, caused administrative inconveniences and threatened the existence of the company's contract.

The bank teller who was rude to the egocentric customer, ended up in unnecessary meetings and writing endless reports needed by managers, directors and the board chairman.

Adopt a positive attitude in all situations.

"True-service is a "heart-orientation" and cannot be well taught if the heart is not fuelled by a desire to serve."

Chapter 11

POLICIES, SYSTEMS, PROCESSES & STANDARDS (PSPS)

"Technology disruptions are also creating an urgent need for innovative customer experiences...Although the impetus is strategic, many businesses don't apply strategic rigor to their customer experience efforts. Instead, they often define customer experience too narrowly as one of many processes ripe for improvement. As a result, investments can fail to move the needle."
—DISNEY INSTITUTE/HBR-AS

IMPORTANCE OF POLICIES, SYSTEMS, PROCESSES AND STANDARDS

The PSPS pillar of the 5-Star Customer Service framework is derived from one of the Keys covered in detail in my book, *"The 3 Keys To Growth, Profits and Sustained Success – How to Build a World-Class Global Business."* It is an essential ingredient for systematising, standardising and evaluating your Customer service strategy and initiatives. This component will make seamless service delivery a reality.

LEARNING QUESTIONS

- Can you identify and list the various Policies, Systems, Processes and Standards which influence the quality of Customer Service offered by your organisation?

- In which elements can you recommend changes to be effected for the improvement of customer service? List 3-5 recommendations and suggestions and share them with your manager or workmates for discussion.

The importance of systems in any business and especially to customer service provision, must be highlighted. In this chapter we focus on Systems and in Chapter 13, we will focus on those issues which may affect the strategy, systems and the quality of service, as a result of the human factor.

CORPORATE POSITIONING FOR 5-STAR CUSTOMER SERVICE

It is scary and sad to notice that, in this day and age, we still have shops with posters hanging on the wall, reading:

"No return, No refund, No exchange"

It reminds me of a major telecommunications company which made a decision to purchase substandard modems from a certain supplier, getting a 3-month warranty. This warranty period was only revealed to clients when the modems began to malfunction within 6 months of purchase. The service provider refused to replace and I am one of the customers who decided to suspend using their service! They opted to lose all potential/future revenue, over a replacement cost that was less than one month's service subscription.

♦ Even if you depend on other service providers to satisfy your customers' needs, you must take and retain ownership of your own customers' happiness.

STANDARDISATION & QUALITY MANAGEMENT

"If.... that huge tiny word. ISO works if you work. Otherwise, it is just another plaque on the wall in reception."
– ROD GOULT

a) ISO (Quality Standard) Certification[9a]

It is the challenge for every service provider, who seeks to implement Quality Management Systems under ISO Standard Certification, to practice and continuously improve, so that value is added to customers and all stakeholders. It must not be a mere wall hanging or a "compliance issue." A summary of the standards under the ISO 9000 family are:

- ISO 9001:2008 - sets out the requirements of a quality management system. The standard has been reviewed and upgraded to ISO 9001:2015.

- ISO 9000:2005 - covers the basic concepts and language.

- ISO 9004:2009 - focuses on how to make a quality management system more efficient and effective.

- ISO 19011:2011 - sets out guidance on internal and external audits of quality management systems.

ISO 9001:2015 - Quality Management System

"ISO 9001 is based on the plan-do-check-act methodology and provides a process-oriented approach to documenting and reviewing the structure, responsibilities, and procedures required to achieve effective quality management in an organization. Specific sections of the standard contain information on topics such as:

- *Requirements for a quality management system, including documentation of a quality manual, document control, and determining process interactions.*
- *Responsibilities of management.*
- *Management of resources, including human resources and an organization's work environment.*

- *Product realization, including the steps from design to delivery.*
- *Measurement, analysis, and improvement of the QMS through activities like internal audits and corrective and preventive action.*
- *...Changes introduced in the 2015 revision are intended to ensure that ISO 9001 continues to adapt to the changing environments in which organizations operate.*
- *Some of the key updates in ISO 9001:2015 include the introduction of new terminology, restructuring some of the information, an emphasis on risk-based thinking to enhance the application of the process approach, improved applicability for services, and increased leadership requirements."* [9b]

- In the ISO 9000 family, this is the only standard to which an organisation can be certified.

- The quality management principles on which this standard is premised include:

    a) Customer-focus.
    b) Serious commitment by senior management.
    c) Adoption of the process approach.
    d) Adherence to continuous improvement strategies.

- The standard helps ensure *"customers get consistent, good quality products and services, which in turn brings many business benefits."*

- Requirements for the organisation include having documented procedures for control of documents, control of records, internal audit, control of nonconforming products, corrective action and preventive action.

- You must put in place a quality manual, a statement of quality policy setting the quality objectives.

- The documentation must be used to help the internal or external audit processes, these determine or identify any areas of Non-conformance (NCs).

- Non-conforming products, services and processes will require corrective action and enable the formulation of preventative action.

- It is the responsibility of senior management to put the customers' needs first – policies and systems which ensure consistent service quality and customer satisfaction must be implemented throughout the operations of the organisation.

- Any large or small organisation can join over one million companies in over 170 countries that effectively use the ISO 9001:2008 (upgrading to 9001:2015) standard.

5-Star Customer Service

- Whilst certification is not mandatory, it adds credibility to the products and services an organisation offers. Other industries and markets can, however, make certification a legal or contractual requirement.

- ISO does not perform certification, but only develops and sells the International Standards. It works with external certification bodies and also assists by producing standards relating to the certification process, through the ISO Committee on Conformity Assessment (CASCO).

- National Standards Bodies (NSBs) like the Standards Association of Zimbabwe (SAZ), Accreditation bodies and Certification bodies are responsible for certification.

- Due to the above, the correct way to denote an organisation's certification is *"ISO 9001:2015 Certified"* and NOT, *"ISO Certified"*

- The role of ISO standards auditors, training bodies and consultants, is important. However, the National Standards body remains a very reliable source of information regarding the requirements of ISO 9001:2015.

"ISO 9001 offers more than quality benefits. The standard should be thought of as a business management tool an organization can use to drive value, improve its operations and reduce its risks."
- OSCAR COMBS, STANDARD WISE

b) Malcolm Baldrige Criteria for Performance Excellence[10]

This American Standard for Performance Excellence, can add value to any 5-Star Service provider committed to implementing management systems based on the seven categories making up the award criteria:

i) Leadership - Examines how senior executives guide and sustain the organization and how the organization addresses Governance, ethical, legal and community responsibilities.

ii) Strategic planning - Examines how the organization sets strategic directions and how it determines and deploys key action plans.

iii) Customer focus - Examines how the organization determines requirements and expectations of customers and markets; builds relationships with customers; and acquires, satisfies, and retains customers.

iv) Measurement, analysis, and knowledge management - Examines the management, use, analysis, and improvement of data and information to support key organization processes as well as how the organization reviews its performance.

v) Workforce focus - Examines how the organization engages, manages, and develops all those actively involved in accomplishing the work of the organization to develop full potential and how the workforce is aligned with the organization's objectives.

vi) Process management - Examines aspects of how key production/delivery and support processes are designed, managed, and improved.

vii) Results - Examines the organization's performance and improvement in its key business areas: customer satisfaction, financial and marketplace performance, workforce, product/service, and operational effectiveness, and leadership. The category also examines how the organization performs relative to competitors.

c) Surveys & Feedback Systems

- **Benchmarking Surveys** – Benchmarking and Performance Review Surveys can help you benchmark the quality of your brand offering against what the best in the world or in your specific market are doing.

- **Performance Review Surveys** – other tools, like Mystery Shopper Surveys, can help you measure and review actual performance, as well as the customer's perception of your service/product offering.

- The use of other feedback systems, like online or printed feedback forms, toll-free contact numbers, customer interviews, suggestion boxes and complaints registers will ensure the organisation constantly receives vital information for use in Quality Control and Continuous Improvement initiatives.

d) Complaints Handling

- Ensure a reliable, effective and easily accessible complaints handling system is in place.

e) Meetings as Facilitators of Excellence

i) Staff Meetings

- Ensure customer service is a key part of the agenda during all scheduled management and operations meetings within the organisation. Meetings can be held as short daily briefs, weekly discussions or full monthly meetings. A combination of these will be suitable depending on the nature and structure of your business.

ii) Stakeholder Meetings

- Interact formally and informally, with your key stakeholders and customers, to ensure you get their input for your Strategy reviews and Continuous Improvement initiatives.

I write on how to make meetings more effective, in the Personal Development book *"Making Success Deliberate."* One big mining house holds key management meetings every Monday morning, if the meeting starts at 8am, the boardroom door is locked at exactly 8am, regardless of who is not yet in. Make sure everyone takes meetings serious and ensure all the hours spent in meetings, count for something.

THE 5-STAR FOCUS ON QUALITY MANAGEMENT SYSTEMS

"A management system describes the set of procedures an organization needs to follow in order to meet its objectives. In some small organizations, there may not be an official system, just "our way of doing things" that is mostly kept in the heads of the staff. But the larger the organization, the more likely that procedures need to be recorded to ensure everyone is clear on who does what. This process of systemizing how things are done is known as a management system."

-ISO

1. **Customer focus** - all efforts and plans must be aimed at understanding, meeting and exceeding customer needs and expectations. Customers are the heart of the organisation, giving it the reason for existence as well as being the source of revenue.

2. **Senior Management commitment** - The organisation's culture is dictated from the practices modelled by senior leadership. The ability of management to simplify and clarify the vision, mission, values and strategic objectives will enable every team member to focus on a common vision. This enables the creation of a high performance team environment and culture required for provision of quality service delivery.

3. **Meaningful Involvement of Key Stakeholders (MIKS)** - Involvement of internal and external customers at all levels makes the goal to provide excellent service quality, more realistic. It is the customers who define what excellent service means to them and taking their input seriously is key in this process.

4. **PSPS approach** - Policies, Systems, Processes and Standards must be aligned and managed to enable effective and efficient execution of the organisation's strategies meant to satisfy customers and attain strategic goals. This approach includes implementation of a Business Management System (BMS) to produce deliberate and seamless product and service quality. Adoption of processes and systems helps to improve objectivity and quality of decision-making.

5-Star Customer Service

5. **Continuous Improvement** - Excellence is not a skill, it's a habit. Your organisation must become a learning and continuously improving organisation – researching and looking at better and new ways of doing business and serving its customers.

LEARNING QUESTIONS

1. When you establish new systems or effect changes to existing ones - who are you making it easier for, to whom are you extending additional convenience? Is it to customers, to your employees or both? If you cannot extend to both, who ends up with the greater benefit?

2. How reflective of customer needs and expectations, are your systems and policies? How much, and at what point, do you consult with your customers and key stakeholders?

3. How empowering are your policies and systems, to adequately resource staff to generate customer experiences that are pleasantly mcmorable?

4. How effective are your meetings, in bringing you to act on issues that will help improve service delivery? What can you do to make your meetings more productive?

PERSONAL SYSTEMS

"The quality of individuals in reflected in the standards they set for themselves"
- RAY CROC

"Be a yardstick of quality. Some people aren't used to an environment where excellence is expected"
-STEVE JOBS

1. A Place for Everything

- Develop your organising skills and make life easier for yourself and your customers by assigning a place for everything.

- Ergonomics - Organise your desk, your electronic and physical files, your wardrobe and all your environments to help you become more efficient and effective.

- This will save you loads of time for allocation to more productive tasks, instead of searching for misplaced items.

2. A Time for Everything

- Your planning skills must be sharpened to enable the effective scheduling of priorities, including the flexibility required to remain responsive to dynamic business and customer needs.

- This will enable a healthy balance of your personal and business demands to enable a perpetual cycle of rejuvenation.

3. A Way for Everything

- The confidence which comes from your in-depth knowledge and technical competences for your line of work, will enable you to craft methods and processes required to deliver quality service and product solutions to meet customer needs.

IMPROVING SERVICE THROUGH TECHNOLOGY

- The initial reaction to long queues, is to celebrate the support received from customers as the market responds to your service or product offering.

- If no responsive action is taken, complaints will eventually come, pointing to your inefficiencies and failure to satisfy customers' expectations.

- The temptation is to open more branches and hire more employees. What can the right deployment of technology, do for you and your customers?

- Employing the right technologies and other strategies can help organisations to serve more customers at lower costs.

Benefits of Technology

1. Enabling the entire organisation to offer seamless customer service, with access to same information.
2. Empowers organisations to serve customers around the globe, with ease.
3. The Q-Busters! – Extending convenience to customers by giving them access to service and information from the comfort of their homes and offices.

Outsourcing of support services

"Never outsource your core competency. If we were trying to build our brand to be about the very best customer service, we knew that we shouldn't be outsourcing that department...To build the Zappos brand into being about the very best customer service, we needed to make sure customer service was the entire company, not just a department."

- TONY HSIEH | CEO, ZAPPOS.COM

STANDARDS AND SYSTEMS MUST HELP THE BUSINESS TO GROW

GROWTH
(INCREASED MARKET SHARE, REVENUE & PROFITABILITY)

=

RETENTION OF EXISTING CUSTOMERS
(5-STAR CUSTOMER SERVICE & CRM)

+

ATTRACTION OF NEW CUSTOMERS
(REFERRALS FROM SATISFIED CUSTOMERS & MARKETING INITIATIVES)

STEPS FROM STRATEGY TO 5-STAR CUSTOMER SERVICE DELIVERY

1. **Strategy Formulation**
   - Vision, Mission and Values must be clearly defined.
   - Strategic Plan needs to reflect Customer Service as a Key Result Area.
   - Non-negotiable involvement of all departments and all levels of staff.

2. **Stakeholder Involvement**
   - Participation and input in Strategy formulation from all key stakeholders.
   - De-politicisation of service and stakeholder participation to promote good corporate governance - Meaningful Involvement of Key Stakeholders (MIKS)
   - Customer Service or Citizen Charter formulation as a shared vision (For use by external parties in the same way a Business Proposal is used)

♦ Customer Service Standards set in line with stakeholders' expectations.

3. **Strategy Execution**
    ♦ Customer Service/Care Plan becomes the basis on which Customer Service strategy is executed. (This is for internal use in the same way the Business Plan, Marketing Plan, Financial Plan (Budget), Operations Plan e.t.c. are meant for the organisation's conceptual direction).
    ♦ Each department must make its own plan that feeds into the consolidated corporate Customer Service Plan.
    ♦ The contents of the Plan are condensed into what is then launched as the Customer Service Charter or Citizen Charter (for Public sector organisations).
    ♦ Details of what goes into the Customer Service Plan and into the Customer Service Charter are covered later in this chapter.

4. **Human Capital Management & Development**
    ♦ Talent Selection, Placement & Development are critical components of the process. Since you cannot separate the service from the one providing it, the quality of the talent you employ will be in direct proportion to the quality of service you offer. *"Your organisation is only as good as the people it employs."*

- Continuous training can assist in improving the elements of programming which influence staff motivation and habits practiced – Beliefs, values, attitudes and feelings. The so-called *"civil servant mentality"* and an unconducive approach to management, work, service delivery and customer care, can and must be addressed. It all starts at the top!

5. Performance Management

- Systems must be in place to ensure employees shift to adopting a *"Practitioner Status"* in their area of specialty.
- Measure your Results against set Standards and Targets – e.g. through Integrated Results Based Management (IRBM), Service Level Benchmarking (SLB), Balanced Score Card or your own internal Performance Management System. Peer-to-Peer Reviews like the SLB must be encouraged, wherever the framework exists.
- Use Customer Surveys and other feedback mechanisms, like interviews and suggestion boxes, to continuously evaluate levels of customer satisfaction as well as identifying areas of improvement.

6. **5-Star Customer Service**
   The processes above should guide the organisation to be deliberate through the programs, initiatives and activities which enable Customer Service to reach 5-Star ratings. Offering full Customer Service attributes:

   - Service/Product Delivery
   - Customer Support
   - Customer Care (Hospitality)

LEARNING QUESTIONS

1. How deliberate is the inclusion of Customer Service in your Strategy?

2. Are you dismissing the Customer Service Pillar, simply because you cannot measure its Return On Investment (ROI)? How can you begin to quantify and measure the ROI on Customer Service and Customer Relationship Management (CRM)?

CUSTOMER SERVICE PLAN

In the 5-Star Customer Service Context/Framework, a customer service plan documents, in greater detail, the organisation's understanding of its internal and external customers' and stakeholders' needs and expectations. It then outlines the strategies and activities it will implement, to align its service delivery and customer care, so it meets the identified customer needs and expectations.

The Customer Service Plan draws its direction from the Strategic Plan, formulated to ensure the organisation realises its Vision, fulfils its Mission and practices its Core Values in order to create the desired organisational Culture - inclusive of 5-Star Customer Service (Service Excellence) and other Key Result Areas.

Other organisations opt to integrate the Customer Service Plan and the Customer Service Charter into a single document and process – there is no rigid approach as it all depends on the needs of each organization and their approach of choice.

What Must Be Included In The Plan

1. Describe the organisation's Customer Service Vision or Philosophy. This must also be done at a departmental or business unit level.

2. Document and continuously update the feedback from customers, regarding their needs, expectations, complaints and recommendations. Sources can be:

   a) Front office staff.
   b) Customers and their representatives.
   c) Surveys, Interviews and feedback forms.

3. Departmental Customer Service SWOT Analysis must be conducted and documented. Example:

   a. **Strengths** - Good product knowledge & technical expertise.

   b. **Weaknesses** – Shortage of staff.

   c. **Opportunities** – Increase in population in need of the residential and business stands you offer.

   d. **Threats** - Political pressure to de-regularise your economic sector.

4. Description of Customer Experiences expected

   a) Flow Charts and Service Area diagrams.

   b) Documented Processes for Service Activities (Examples – What is expected when customer visits the service office? When staff go to collect meter readings? When there is a fault or a customer registers a complaint? When the customer hasn't paid on due date? When a customer is emotional – angry, bereaved, stressed e.t.c?)

EXAMPLES OF SERVICE FACTORS & STANDARDS

"Quality in service or products is not what you put into it. It is what the client or customer gets out of it."
-PETER DRUCKER-

i. **Reception**
- Customers must be greeted with a friendly, welcoming smile and politely asked how they may be assisted.
- Look at the customer while you greet/acknowledge them with a smile.
- Seats must be available for waiting customers.

ii. **Waiting Time**
- Customers in queue to be served within 3 minutes.
- Every customer to get help, acknowledgement or attention within the 1st minute of approaching service area.

iii. **Office Appearance**
- All offices must be cleaned every day and dust bins emptied at least twice a day.
- Clean-desk policy – proper filing and desk arrangement.

iv. Staff Appearance
- Office staff to be in formal clothing with jacket and tie from Monday to Thursday, except when going for field assignments.
- Dress down in smart casual on Fridays and Saturdays. (Clearly define *'dress down'*)
- Workshop staff to be in proper and full PPE.

v. Telephone Calls
- Phones should be answered within 3 rings.
- Greet customer with Appreciation, Introduce Company and Yourself.
- Politely ask how you may help.
- Assist with a Positive Attitude and Summarise agreed action plan.
- Thank the customer and hang up last.

vi. Complaints Handling
- Every department to avail complaints register, which customers can easily access without any form of discomfort.
- Complaints to be acknowledged with 48 hours.
- Resolution plan or feedback on progress to be made within 72 hours of receipt of complaint.

vii. Customer Feedback

- Customer suggestion boxes must be in place at all service points.
- Email address, telephone (preferably toll-free) and Whatsapp numbers to be provided for customer feedback.
- All issues requiring feedback to customers must be acknowledged or responded to, within 7 days of opening suggestion box or emails.
- Emails and Suggestion boxes to be opened and processed at least once every day and twice every week, respectively.

viii. Accessibility & Availability/Working Hours

- Stagger lunch/tea breaks in all service areas to ensure customers get uninterrupted service throughout the day. Where possible invest in 24/7/365 Service Call Centre.
- All office buildings, ablution facilities and offices to be friendly to physically challenged customers and visitors.
- All key service phone numbers and email addresses to be displayed at reception area for each department.
- Display working hours, where customers can easily notice.

ix. Dealing with Suppliers

- Ensure adequate induction of all suppliers, including provision of requirements, payment terms and thorough understanding of your business and needs/expectations.
- Give adequate time for order fulfilment and advise when they can expect to get paid, per order terms.
- Ensure order confirmation advice is issued before service or product is delivered.
- Always communicate any changes to agreed terms and conditions, even if it means they may be disappointed. Don't lie to them or wait for them to complain – consider them your important partners.

x. Vital Delivery Information

- Advise standard or indicative expected time or period customers should expect delivery.
- Provide specifications of product or service description, quality or workmanship.
- Offer other useful customer educational, product use or handling information.

5. Customer Service Improvement Strategies

Consider the following, for discussion and possible improvement of your organisation's Customer Service:

a) Process Improvement
- Designing user-friendly forms.
- Policies requiring improvement to enhance customer experiences.
- Customer Service review meetings.
- Collection of revenue and engaging debtors.
- Service to suppliers.

b) Impressions/Image
- Provision of uniform or clothing allowance.
- Employment of cleaning service providers.
- Branding excellence.

c) Knowledge & Skills
- Standard 5-Star Customer Service training as part of Induction of new employees.
- Annual customer care refresher workshops for existing employees.
- Monthly departmental meetings.
- Weekly sectional meetings and Daily morning briefing meetings.
- Corporate library with recommended text for each level of employees, including feedback and review sessions.

d) Service Delivery Methods
- Communication and customer engagement for input to product development or improvement processes.
- Tech-based payment and service access platforms. Including account statements.
- Increased convenience – self-service or direct deliveries.
- Quality improvement and reduced delivery time and cost.

e) Staff Motivation
- Verbal praise.
- Employee of the Month certificates.
- Appreciation gifts - shopping vouchers, fuel coupons, time off, dinner out, medals, trophies, bonuses.
- Point system feeding into Performance management and remuneration framework.

Chapter 12

SYSTEMATISING SERVICE DELIVERY IN PUBLIC INSTITUTIONS

"As public services are funded by citizens, either directly or indirectly through taxes, they have the right to expect a particular quality of service that is responsive to their needs and is provided efficiently at a reasonable cost."
–CENTRE FOR GOOD GOVERNANCE, INDIA

CITIZEN/CUSTOMER SUPPORT & SERVICE DELIVERY (CSSD) STRATEGIES FOR PUBLIC SECTOR SERVICE PROVIDERS

One of the most frequently asked questions during our training sessions has always been:

"When are you going to train the government and other public service providers, on how to treat us as important customers?"

In the introduction to this book I mentioned the responses, given by two senior executives, to my request for information on how they were handling customer service and CRM. There was a clear display of a limited appreciation of Customer Service principles and the contributions that the best organisations can make. I then challenged that you imagine an executive with such a view, being appointed to become a government minister or senior public official. What Service Culture or quality would you expect to prevail in the ministries or departments such executives will be leading?

It has been encouraging that baby-steps have been made over the years and if partners involved in the initiatives to make public-sector service providers more customer and citizen-focused, continue investing in and supporting these critical areas – we will be able to see and feel the difference as citizens and customers. Many governments, through-out the world, have realized the need to address service delivery issues and are now partnering with developmental institutions and civil society organizations to build the capacity of government departments and local authorities to be able to offer excellent service.

Over the years, our company has been involved in the implementation of human capital development investments and initiatives in the public sector. This has included 5-Star Customer Service training workshops, facilitation of stakeholder engagement forums, strategic planning and citizen charter formulation, under various Customer/Citizen Support & Service Delivery (CSSD) programs.

The work done by the Government of Zimbabwe in partnership with and funding from development partners like Australian Aid, the World Bank Group and their implementing partners, including UNICEF, World Vision, Mvuramanzi Trust, GIZ, Africare and many others, has made a lot of positive difference in this critical service sector. I am privileged to have been a part of this process and am excited about what this means to the future of service delivery in Zimbabwe.

LEARNING STORY – CHANGE IN PUBLIC SECTOR SERVICE DELIVERY

I literally got goose bumps during a discussion session with representatives of various local authorities. I was shocked at the allegations that some organisations were turning training opportunities into extra-cash earning projects. If a course did not provide access to meaningful allowances, junior staff would be sent to attend, but if there was a nice venue and good allowances, regardless of course objectives and targeted audience – senior management would make sure they were the ones who attended. It was no longer about acquiring knowledge, skills and the opportunity to expand useful professional networks – it was all about the money.

I was later encouraged, when I interacted with the leadership team (management and council) for a small town, on another training program. Change is a process, but I believed they were going in the right direction to take their organisation and community to the desired vision for a City-status. They even created opportunities for the development of junior managers, staff and stakeholder representatives, so everyone could share the same vision and speak the same language towards improvement of service delivery and customer care.

LEARNING STORY[11] – Bulawayo, The City of Kings.

In recent years, the Ministry of Local Government, Rural and Urban Development has awarded Bulawayo City Council with the Water Award as well as the Overall Best Performing Local Authority in Zimbabwe. Bulawayo also came second in the Awards given to Southern African local authorities at a SADC level.

Below, is an account of one of the projects we were involved with, in training over 800 employees for Bulawayo City Council, after which the local authority became the first to launch a Citizen Charter and a Service Call Centre.

"The AusAID – World Vision Bulawayo Water and Sanitation Response Program (BOWSER) program addressed vulnerability to the threat of waterborne diseases by focusing on improved sewerage and water supply systems, and on capacity building to restore the Bulawayo Council's financial sustainability. The $10.1 million program (AusAID contributed $9.1 million and World Vision contributed $1 million) was AusAID Zimbabwe's largest NGO-delivered water, sanitation and hygiene (WASH) program.

It produced impressive results: it reached over 450,000 people and led to a 40 per cent reduction in diarrheal diseases in all age groups; promoted trilateral engagement with South Africa; and supported the establishment of the first municipal Call Centre in Zimbabwe. Key lessons from the project were presented at the 6th World Urban Forum in Naples, Italy in 2012 and at various WASH fora in Zimbabwe.

BOWSER was unusual in its emphasis on urban, rather than rural populations. Phase 1 of BOWSER focused on water, sanitation, critical infrastructure rehabilitation and participatory health and hygiene. Phase 2 consolidated these gains and also supported computer system upgrades and the improvement of council institutional capacity, responsiveness to emergencies and improved service delivery and increased collected revenue...

BOWSER was aligned to the Zimbabwe Government's 2011–2015 National Hygiene and Sanitation Strategy. Concurrently, the program directly addressed two of the objectives of AusAID's WASH program: improving access for the poor to water, sanitation and hygiene facilities; and improving governance to ensure the sustainability of water and sanitation systems in small and medium-sized towns." [11]

Bulawayo City Council has become a shining example of 5-Star Local Governance and public service delivery and frequently hosts other local authorities, as a way of sharing their experience and exchanging ideas to improve service delivery to communities across the African continent.

CITIZEN CHARTERS & CUSTOMER SERVICE CHARTERS[12]

What is a Charter?[12a]

1. **It is a statement of rights and responsibilities:** a formal written statement describing the rights and responsibilities of an organization, local authority or government arm and its customers, stakeholders and/or its citizens

2. **It is the expression of an understanding between the citizen and the public service provider about the quantity and quality of services citizens receive in exchange for their taxes.** It is essentially about the rights of the public and the obligations of the public servants as well as expectations from the citizens

Citizen Charter - Basic Concept, Origin and Principles[12b]

"As public services are funded by citizens, either directly or indirectly through taxes, they have the right to expect a particular quality of service that is responsive to their needs and is provided efficiently at a reasonable cost. The Citizen's Charter is a written, voluntary declaration by service providers about service standards, choice, accessibility, non-discrimination, transparency and accountability. It should be in accordance with the expectations of citizens. Therefore, it is a useful way of defining to customers the nature of service provision and explicit standards of service delivery."
  -CITIZEN CHARTER HANDBOOK, CENTRE FOR
    GOOD GOVERNANCE, INDIA

Lessons From The United Kingdom Initiative[12b]

The concept of Citizen Charters was introduced by Prime Minister of the United Kingdom, John Major's administration in 1991. This followed the thrust for privatisation of state enterprises by Prime Minister Margaret Thatcher's administration, as part of the New Public Management reforms. The privatisation drive was meant to allow the market forces of demand and supply, to dictate issues such as price and quality of service, with the aim to bring customer satisfaction.

In the year of implementation, 28 Citizen Charters were submitted and approved. In the year that followed, 1992, out of over 300 applicants from the public service, the Prime Minister awarded 36 Charter Marks (Awards of Excellence in delivering public service). The Charter was to be fully implemented over a 10 year period.

Since then, many countries have launched Citizen Charters or similar initiatives under different names. These initiatives can be traced to public service improvements in the UK and in other countries like Belgium, France, Argentina, Australia, Canada, the United States, Belgium, Singapore, Hong Kong (Performance Pledge), Malaysia, South African, Jamaica, Namibia, Costa Rica, Samoa, Italy, Portugal, the Netherlands. Zimbabwe's efforts have started with the implementation of Customer Service Charters. The initiatives will require a centralised control and the enforcing authority of an Act of Parliament, to become more effective.

5-Star Customer Service

Over the years, India has gone all-out, implementing Citizen Charters in hundreds of federal and state departments and state owned enterprises, with differing levels of success and drawing some important learning points.

A Citizen Charter is a public policy:
1. To give citizens more power in the market place
2. To raise the standard of public service
3. To improve -
    a) choice
    b) quality
    c) value
    d) accountability
4. NOT intended for government interference in the market place.

The Citizen Charter is expected to promote the following Principles in relation to Service:
  a) Quality
  b) Choice
  c) Standards
  d) Value for money
  e) Accessibility
  f) Information
  g) Complaints handling
  h) Accountability
  i) Non-discrimination or (what I call), Meaningful Involvement of Key Stakeholders (MIKS)

The spirit behind the Citizen Charter must be:
1. to put the customer first
2. to recognise good service
3. to expose incompetence

5-Star Customer Service

In the public sector and state owned enterprises (SOEs) or parastatals, products and services are paid for by the public through direct or indirect taxes, levies and service fees/charges. They are not free services, therefore customers expect:

1. High-quality goods and services
2. Value for money – whichever way each customer defines this
3. Responsiveness to their needs and expectations
4. Efficient service at a reasonable cost
5. Service provided fairly, effectively and courteously

Why we need Citizen or Customer Service Charters

"A further rationale for the Charters is to help change the mind-set of the public official from someone with power over the public to someone with care of duty in spending the public money collected through taxes and in providing them with necessary services."
 -CITIZEN CHARTER HANDBOOK, CENTRE FOR GOOD GOVERNANCE, INDIA

If effectively implemented the benefits of Charters include:

- Giving the public service providers a sense of pride and satisfaction.
- Ensuring customers receive quality service and the power to influence decisions affecting them.

CONTENTS OF A CHARTER

The Citizen Charter can be as short as one page, and can include any or all of the following:

1. Mission, Vision, Values of your organisation.
2. Definition of a Charter.
3. The Products and Services you offer.
4. Identification of your Customers.
5. How Your Customers can Help You serve them better – you can ask your customers to help you by doing any of the following, depending on your nature of business:
   a) Treating your staff courteously and respectfully
   b) Providing feedback which enables you to improve the service you give them
   c) Providing accurate information in their dealings with you.
   d) Making any payments due from them in time.
   e) Keep a record of important documents and correspondences related to their dealings with you.
   f) Make their complaints clear by providing all necessary details like names or offices concerned, what exactly transpired, the date and time as well as how they are expecting the complaint to be resolved. To avail any past correspondence or receipts if that will help quickly get to the solution.
   g) Comply with any legitimate requests for information or documents that will help you serve them or respond to their complaints better.

5-Star Customer Service

6. Other elements your customers should expect from you:
   a) Their meaningful involvement (MIKS)
   b) Privacy and Confidentiality
7. How customers can get access to your products and services.
8. How customers can make complaints, if they are not satisfied, including:
   a) Clearly communicated Complaints redress procedures.
   b) Inform customers of their right to complain, should they not be happy with the service or product provided.
   c) Advise the standard they should expect so they know what to complain about and when.
   d) Advise customers on how, to whom and where to register their complaint – e.g. starting with the person who served them, then their supervisor and thereafter the manager etc.
   e) How the complaint will be dealt with and with whom they can follow-up.
   f) How they will know their complaint is being attended to.
   g) Time it will take to resolve the complaint.
   h) Advise them of the procedure for appeals, whenever they are not happy with how their complaint has been resolved.
9. Communication

   The Charter must be clear about how you will be handling communication with your customers:

a) Your commitment to deal with enquiries promptly and in a helpful, courteous and responsive way.
b) Staff identifying themselves by name, especially when answering the telephone.
c) Standard time frame for acknowledgement of written communication like letters and emails.
d) Your standard for answering the telephone, including response time and how the phone must be answered.
e) Procedure for feedback mechanisms like suggestion boxes and tip-offs, as well as how responses will be managed.
f) All responses to customers to provide name and contact details of the person or department handling the complaint.

The Steps to a Service or Citizen Charter

1. Ensure meaningful involvement of consuming customer representatives, citizen associations, key stakeholders and employee representatives from all the key areas within the organisation.
2. Engagement of an expert to train stakeholders and facilitate stakeholder meetings.
3. Formulation and alignment of sectional, departmental and group charters.
4. A representative Steering Committee must be set-up to be the Project Management team for the entire exercise.
5. Identify and list all Stakeholders and major services and products offered by your organisation.

6. Prepare the Draft Charter
   a) Circulation for comments/suggestions
   b) Modification of Charter to include suggestions.
7. Send the Charter for consideration, modification and endorsement by the parent authority, whether the board of directors or the ministry/department.
8. Get approval by the Minister-in-charge or the Board.
9. Submit a copy of the charter to other relevant authorities.
10. Launching of the Charter with generous promotion and publicity strategies and events, including posters, website and other print and electronic media. All efforts must ensure the market becomes aware of the Charter's existence.
11. Monitoring and evaluation of the Charters, using both internally and external review/audit processes.
12. Utilise results from surveys and reports from reviews to ensure a continuous improvement approach.

THE CONDITIONS FOR SUCCESS

- As the organisation goes through all the steps above, the guidance of an experienced person in this area, remains critical.
- Proper training and engagement of staff and key stakeholders are non-negotiable requirements.

- Reasons for failure include lack of knowledge, lack of expert training and guidance for those responsible in crafting and implementing the charter.

The following can be done, to bring success:

a) Shift in HR policies on Recruitment, Selection and Training. Employ the best qualified and the best attitude.
b) Change in culture - driven from the top.
c) Continuous CSSD and Customer Care Training.
d) Effective Performance Management Systems.
e) Upgrading systems and promoting use of new, relevant technologies to improve service.
f) A demanding citizen – it's not free service, customers pay through direct and indirect taxes. (Refer to the Limiters of Excellent Service - demanding customers who speak out and commend).
g) Participation and meaningful involvement of stakeholders and staff who interact with external customers.
h) Managing By Walking Around (MBWA) – leaders and managers must never lose a connection with the reality on the ground. They must have a personal reality of what customers are experiencing and the quality of service they are receiving.

i) Availability of funds and other resources, for research, benchmarking, and implementation of programs promoting service excellence.

j) De-politicising service delivery in local authorities, parastatals and government departments – focus on TLC principles, by thinking about those you serve and exist for.

- For success and effectiveness, Charters must not be implemented to please donors, but to improve service delivery through excellence in public administration and governance. If you focus on the latter and do it well, even the donors will be more than impressed.

- Constitute a panel of technical and expert advisors at a national level and for each key sector. Put in place a process for independent review and audit, with quarterly and annual reports made available to the public. Independent audits must be carried out to ensure transparency, fairness and objectivity in the review processes.

- Reports on service audits and surveys must be made public, so customers know how well they are being served.

- Introduce competition between private and public sector, by liberalising or opening up part of the services that were only restricted to public institutions. Allow private service providers to offer those services and compare results as well as allow the market to choose on the basis of service quality.

- To improve customer, investor and stakeholder confidence and satisfaction, introduce performance-based reward systems in public institutions.

- Adopt a sectoral approach to improve effectiveness and trace what each sector is doing, including customising expected service standards. Examples of sector categories could be:

  1. Health
  2. Education
  3. Energy
  4. Postal & Telecommunications
  5. Media – Print, Radio and TV
  6. Others like Public Service Admin, Financial Services, Agriculture, Mining etc

- Establish information centres or call centres for each sector or organisation.

- Establish Citizen Charters as and through an Act of Parliament, for enforcement in all public sector organisations.

- Have a National Annual Report on Service Delivery

- Ensure there are Effective Consumer/Customer Councils and Associations:
  a) Consumer Council
  b) Standards Association

c) The Ombudsman or Public Protector
d) Surveys, Research and Statistics (e.g. Zimstats etc)
e) Ensure Charters become a National Service Contract for all Sectors
f) Monitor and evaluate performance against set standards
g) Produce periodic and annual reports publicised nationally

PUBLIC INSTITUTIONS CAN DO MORE:

1. Make their services easily accessible through multi-channels, including service centres and websites.
2. Ensure access to the clients account statement and other information through secure online platforms.
3. Publicise the different ways through which customers can easily and conveniently contact the organisation.
4. Enable all services that can be accessed through technological platforms are availed as self-service options.
5. Engage customers through the Virtual Meeting Places (Social Media platforms)
6. Set up efficient 24-hour call centre facilities to ensure timely response to emergencies and extended convenience to customers.
7. Avail toll-free contact details and other communication channels like Whatsapp.
8. Have dedicated enquiries counters or desks as well as training all staff in product knowledge to empower everyone to better serve customers

with useful information about the organisation and its services.
9. Train staff in 5-Star Customer service knowledge and skills.
10. Focus on identifying and meeting customer needs.
11. Improve forms, documents and procedures to make them more customer-friendly and customer-focused.
12. Conduct surveys, investigate complaints and use findings to improve quality of customer service experiences.
13. Keep a record of all complaints or queries attended to and report on monthly, quarterly and annual performance on this key focus area. Use the statistics and findings to set and review performance targets.
14. Deal with bureaucratic processes and depoliticise service delivery
15. The UK government had a realistic timeframe of 10 years to fully implement Citizen Charters and derive expected benefits. Goal and targets set must be realistic, without the pressure of expecting results over-night.
16. The move from a comfort zone to doing things differently will always come with some level of stress, pain and consequently, some form of resistance. Consistency and persistency must remain key to enable sustainable culture change.

LEARNING QUESTIONS

1. As a leader or manager, what level of stewardship are you reflecting in your service to those who depend on your organisation?

2. How responsibly, are you using your power, to make a positive difference?

WHAT THE BEST IN THE WORLD ARE DOING

REMEMBER: Whilst the drive is to have Customer Service Charters in place, organisations must never lose focus of the goal to turn the Contents of the Charter, into a Culture they Practice daily to provide 5-Star Customer Service to all stakeholders.

Exemplary implementation of the Citizen's Charter by Banks in India[12b]

In India, three major institutions in the Banking Sector were selected to build a model of excellence in the implementation of the Citizen's Charter in 2000. The process included stakeholder involvement, meaningful involvement of staff, creating awareness and specialised training for all levels of employees regarding the citizen charter concept and the implementation process. Train-the-trainer type of programs were implemented for effective roll-out of training activities.

Review and evaluation of effectiveness was conducted by independent agencies, and corrective action plans implemented. Each bank's charter was revised and aligned with the Bankers' Association charter. On completion of the launch and implementation roll-out, external experts were engaged to evaluate the implementation of the Citizen Charters by the banks.

- There will be a need to identify the best sectors or institutions in which to run pilot programs, as part of the implementation learning process.

- Each organisation serving the public, must be challenged to act and practice 5-Star Customer Service principles.

- The right attitude and level of commitment, are the bridge required to move from conferences and policies on paper, to practice and a culture of performance excellence.

LEARNING QUESTIONS

1. Do you know of any organised efforts being made in your area (town or city), to improve service delivery through the formulation and implementation of Citizen or Customer Service Charters? What are the challenges in making this a reality?

2. Is there a living and active Customer Service Charter for your organisation? List all your key stakeholders and customers. How many of them were afforded the opportunity to contribute towards the crafting of your Service Charter?

3. How can you start turning your Service Charter, from a dead wall plaque, into a vibrant tool in guiding the practice of a 5-Star Customer Service Culture within your organisation?

4. How frequently do you review and evaluate your performance against the commitments expressed through your Service Charter?

Chapter 13

CUSTOMER RELATIONSHIP MANAGEMENT & TEAM DYNAMICS

"40% of customers say that "Better Human Service" is the most requested improvement from companies."
– GENESYS GLOBAL SURVEY

CUSTOMER RELATIONSHIP MANAGEMENT

The word customer comes from *custom* – meaning, when people make it a habit, a tradition, a routine or a custom, to give you their business - they become your *customers*. They can only do this when you invest in understanding them better and building genuine relationships with them.

The purpose of good Customer Relationship Management (CRM) is to create a Personalised Experience for each customer, demonstrating your thorough understanding of them and their needs. This will lead to Customer Loyalty, repeat business and new business referred by your loyal customers, because they trust you to deliver. It is an effective tool for sustaining business growth.

"Customer relationship management (CRM) typically involves tracking individual customer behaviour over time, and using this knowledge to configure solutions precisely tailored to the customers' and vendors' needs."

In the context of choice, this implies designing longitudinal models of choice over the breadth of the firm's products and using them prescriptively to increase the revenues from customers over their lifecycle. Several factors have recently contributed to the rise in the use of CRM in the marketplace:

- *A shift in focus in many organizations, towards increasing the share of requirements among their current customers rather than fighting for new customers.*
- *An explosion in data acquired about customers, through the integration of internal databases and acquisition of external syndicated data.*
- *Computing power is increasing exponentially.*
- *Software and tools are being developed to exploit these data and computers, bringing the analytical tools to the decision maker, rather than restricting their access to analysts.*

Analytical customer relationship management (CRM) is the process of collecting and analyzing a firm's information regarding customer interactions in order to enhance the customers' values to the firm.

Firms exploit such information by designing strategies uniquely targeted to consumer needs. This process enhances loyalty and increases switching costs, as information on consumer preferences affords an enduring competitive advantage. By integrating various data (e.g. across purchases, operations, service logs, etc.), choice researchers can obtain a more complete view of customer behaviour. These developments cut across industries, including banking, telephony, Internet, and other areas that have received limited attention in the marketing literature. In addition, each industry likely has unique challenges of its own.

Analytical CRM involves using firms' data on its customers to design longitudinal models of choice over the breadth of the firm's products and using them prescriptively to increase the revenues from customers over their lifecycle. In contrast, ***behavioural CRM uses experiments and surveys to focus upon the psychological underpinnings of the service interaction, or the managerial structures that make CRM effective.***[13]

PRINCIPLES OF CUSTOMER RELATIONSHIP MANAGEMENT (CRM)

In the 5-Star Customer Service Model, the basis for Team and Customer Relationship Management, is enabled by understanding customers and their needs as set out under the Knowledge and Skills Star as well as the Know Your Customer (KYC) systems covered under the PSPS Star. The need to leverage technology to manage relationships is covered under the Effective Communication and the PSPS Stars. The Attitude & Personal Brand Development Star ensures effective interpersonal skills vital for developing both internal and external relationships.

The above can give you a clue, to the reason why the Customer Relationship Management Star is the fifth and last in the 5-Star Customer Service Model.

5-Star Customer Service

THE 3 PILLARS OF CRM

Define Your Own CRM Strategy and Purpose

As you define your own CRM strategy, make sure you are guided by the pillars that support an effective Customer Relationship Management framework:

- Strategy
- People
- Systems & Technology

These three pillars reflect the basis on which the book, *"The 3 Keys to Growth, Profits & Sustained Success,"* has been written. In this book, the pillars are only covered to the extent they can be applied to help you design an effective CRM Strategy.

1. STRATEGY

Like everything else in your organisation, your CRM Strategy must feed from your overall corporate strategy. Your vision, mission, values and strategic objectives must guide the focus and structure of your CRM initiatives. In this Chapter, we will focus more on the People & CRM Technology systems - for more detail on the process of Strategy to 5-Star Service Delivery, refer to what we covered under Chapter 11.

2. THE 'PEOPLE' FACTOR

"40% of customers say that "Better Human Service" is the most requested improvement from companies."
GENESYS GLOBAL SURVEY

The set-up of your organisation may dictate that you pose more questions, but the following three questions can help you begin looking at the detail of your own "people factor" requirements:

a) Do you have the right people on your team?

b) Are you employing the best management and leadership approach?

c) Is your team well-resourced, well-positioned and motivated?

Genuinely evaluating your organisation against the questions above and addressing any identified gaps, will help you move in the right direction for crafting an effective CRM Strategy. Let's cover each of the three questions:

a) The Right People

"Your organisation, is only as good as the people it employs."

- The Quality Control aspect of 5-Star Customer Service and CRM starts with identifying the right talent for your organisation.
- The quality of your selection process will have a direct influence on the quality of talent you will employ. This includes the job profiling and description done at a departmental level, interviewing model adopted and the proper training of the selectors. A systematised process will ensure recruitment remains objective and professional, not just left to the prejudiced opinion of individuals, who might have vested interests.
- The culture and attitude elements must never be ignored in favour of, only the technical qualifications of, the candidate meant for a CRM role. Forcing the Training department to try and impart these elements to an individual is, in most cases, an expensive (and sometimes futile) exercise.
- Define the attitude you are looking for, just like you define the other aspects of the job and prospect profile.
- The GIGO (Garbage In, Garbage Out) principle applies. Be careful how you choose your CRM team members and everyone else who will ensure service is delivered to your customers.

- The Qualities of a 5-Star Performer fit for CRM responsibilities include the following:

    i. A positive attitude.
    ii. Respect for customers.
    iii. Knowledge of 5-Star Customer service principles.
    iv. Professionally responsive to customer needs & requests.
    v. Planning & organising skills, including time management.
    vi. Analytic and problem solving skills.
    vii. High level of Emotional Intelligence and excellent interpersonal skills.

b) Leadership & Management Approach

- If your recruitment and selection process is of 5-Star quality as indicated above, it means you must be doing the same, or even more, in choosing the right calibre of managers and corporate leaders. Additional tools and focus areas are needed in hiring new managers or developing and promoting existing employees into leadership responsibilities.
- The organisational culture you want to create, in line with your vision, mission and strategic intents, must direct you to the leadership model and approach you need to be adopted by your CRM leaders. Having 5-Star Performers being led by 3-Star Leaders,

- The Qualities of a 5-Star Leader fit for CRM responsibilities include the following:

   i. Excellent team building capabilities.
   ii. Coaching and mentorship skills.
   iii. High level of confidence and professionalism, required to enable effective delegation and empowerment of subordinates.
   iv. High level of Emotional Intelligence.
   v. Negotiation and Problem solving skills.
   vi. Situational leadership.
   vii. Interpersonal & Social skills.
   viii. Ability to practice and inculcate 5-Star Customer Service principles.

c) Placement, Development & Motivation

- Developing a CRM Team, capable of delivering 5-Star Customer Service and guarantee customer loyalty, is linked to your organisation's ability to place people appropriately, expose them to the necessary training and development programs, and employing innovative motivation strategies for sustaining positive attitudes.
- When you have taken time to profile and identify the strengths and capabilities of your Star-Performers, you must then make

an effort to place them in the rightful positions, where they can practice their skill as if it was their 'second nature.' This means involving them, in coming up with the decision of what role they play, with clarity of what is expected of them.

- Expose your talent to quality training programs, which equip and inspire them to be the best practitioners of Customer Service and CRM knowledge and skills. Align these training programs to your Succession Planning framework and their Personal/Professional Development Plans. A fusion of internal and external courses is essential for adequate exposure.
- Build a corporate library and stock it with the best material to feed the culture of performance excellence you need to create.
- Each team member needs to have a clearly spelt-out Career Path Development plan (CPD), and a mentor assigned to coach them as they learn and practice to become the best at their professional game. This must be a plan, which includes specific training programs to complete, books to read and scheduled periodic discussions with the assigned mentor. The mentor can be their immediate manager or someone else, as shall be dictated by the direction of their CPD.
- Use awards and other non-monetary incentives, to motivate your team. It will be most ideal, if their performance can be linked to

your Performance management system, your Succession planning framework and your remuneration/reward system. Creating a great working environment and being a great manager to work with, can be sources of motivation in proportions you would never imagine.

- Build and Lead your team like you want to win a world contest in Customer Service and CRM. Learn from how the great sports/football team coaches do it. Scout for talent, train your talent, reward your talent, celebrate your talent and create the opportunities for them to play and shine. Always offer your coaching services from the side lines (demonstrating how it's done during training sessions) and enjoy the credit as it comes back to you.

LEARNING STORY

One of my former employers asked me to leave the training management role and head another business unit. Two different executives briefed me on my new assignment, and they both warned about one of the *"problem employees."* They no longer knew how to handle her, and they were certain I was going to have problems working with her. I took their advice, but decided to take an open-mind approach. I have always found it easier to build my own relationships, because people respond differently to each one of us.

I focused on each person's strengths and discovered that the *"problem employee"* was an outgoing character who enjoyed socialising and interacting with people. She was stuck in administration work and quite frustrated. We discussed about this in our one-on-one sessions, and agreed that she tries using her skills on the sales team. Indeed she gave me a bit of work managing some unauthorised leave, but within 3 months, she was bringing the best sales results.

She was now properly placed, excited about work again and producing great results. She sent me an email a few years ago, thanking me and advising of her promotion to a Sales Executive position with her new employer.

LEARNING QUESTIONS

1. Do you have the right people serving your customers? Have you identified their strengths and how well positioned are they to be able to give you the best results?
2. Can you identify the CRM qualities that are still lacking within your team and your personal brand? How can you begin to develop those professional qualities?

3. Evaluate whether you are not standing in the way of 5-Star Customer Service because you are afraid, if you develop your team, you might end up being replaced.
4. What is your "people factor" strategy? How are you or can you, develop your team into a 5-Star CRM Team?

Sharing the Team Vision

It is not enough to have 5-Star Players who cannot *'gel-together'* into a 5-Star Team.

Culture is the habitual demonstration and practice of beliefs, values, attitudes, knowledge and skills, constituting the common practices of a group of people or an organisation, over a prolonged period of time. When a team is properly selected, placed and focused to achieve a clearly defined vision, creating a culture of performance excellence becomes possible.

LEARNING STORY

I had another privilege of being asked to transfer from head office, to lead a retail banking branch which had faced a series of challenges that negatively affected its growth; like an award-winning coach in competitive sports, I started working on my team, first – the composition, positioning and development of the team. I took the shortest possible time, to study each individual's strengths, qualifications, passion and learning opportunities.

I scouted for talent, internally and externally. I availed myself as a Personal Development Partner for each team member, shared as much information as I could and created the opportunity for them to grow and shine.

My secretary began her training in clerical duties, eventually becoming a teller, whilst I got a new secretary from another department. We got our customer service supervisor promoted into operations management and another customer service officer promoted to back-office supervision. I head-hunted two new customer service officers from different banks, within the same market and an additional one from another branch. The driver was developed to become a clerk, and eventually a teller and we got the replacement from the best attitude I had met at a retailing business across the street.

We shared the vision of the branch we wanted to create, starting from current performance and how we intended to make the money, whilst pleasing our customers. We were going to be about service excellence and grow by building genuine solid relationships to develop a loyal customer base. In our first meetings, I was always upfront with my wish, to have one of them replace me whenever I finally decided to leave for other opportunities.

It was a real blast. New business started coming, existing customers referred their associates and we had clients walk across from other larger financial institutions they had been exclusively banking with for more than three decades. Within a period of four months, the branch was operating at a profit.

Have a Positive Attitude & Develop Relationship management staff

- Develop the attitude of a Relationship Manager.
- Invest in relevant Training and Development programs on CRM for all staff levels.
- Go beyond the rewards and be able to inspire the team to produce results.
- 5-Star CRM becomes the safety-net during crises – use relationships, loyalty and the trust built over time, to navigate through tough times. Every business that has survived a major crisis, has done so, largely on the back of a loyal customer base.
- Go beyond the workplace and engage with both customers and employees in their own world. At ExtraCity Luxury, the company has initiated innovative team building activities, including those with the spouses of the crew members. This has helped the spouses to better appreciate the nature of

work and travelling schedules of their partners, thereby strengthening all key relationships.

What do you, and your team believe in, when it comes to the link between customer service and team work?

Executive Commitment To Excellence

- Strategic and Executive management commitment to service excellence – strictness in grooming and deportment, backed by investment in training and availing of budgeted requirements should be enforced right from the top.
- For years, this has been demonstrated practically and effectively by Medical Investments Ltd (Avenues Clinics, Montagu and St. Clements Clinics). This has enabled their Certification and re-Certification under the ISO Quality Management Standards, through continuous investment in staff training and development as well as process improvement.
- Culture is driven from the top – senior management commitment must be very clear and visible in both practice and resource allocation.
  - The Deputy Managing Director at one of my former employers, was very strict on issues contributing to a culture of performance and service excellence. A manager would be

asked to go home and return with a clean shave and proper attire (full suit) as required and stipulated by the organisation. Anyone who felt they had an acceptable reason for not attending a course they were scheduled to attend, had to get authorisation for non-attendance, direct from his desk! The organisation ended up with a culture we were all proud to be a part of.

How obsessed is your senior management with 5-Star customer service?

Tony Hsieh, at Zappos.com bragged, and challenged his peers about his organisation's customer service culture – they called one of their service agents, asking the online shoe retailer for help ordering a pizza in the middle of the night. The person who entertained this unusual request, had fun serving the caller, entertaining any questions or conversation by customers and ended up locating and advising the nearest pizza delivery service nearest to the caller.

3. CRM SYSTEMS & TECHNOLOGIES

Know Your Customer (KYC)

There is a growing move to regulate the requirements for each business to improve knowledge of its customers. This has been witnessed in various industries, including banks, air transportation, telecommunications companies and hotels. The regulatory requirements and purpose are, however, not adequate to equip service providers with a 5-Star CRM framework.

KYC initiatives are an important foundation, if purposefully utilised to enhance the quality of service experiences extended to customers. If you keep customer files, records or a database with their personal information, photographs and type of products they consume, you have a good starting point for your CRM strategy.

You are getting left behind, if the only reason you hold that information is to use it when the authorities come to audit your systems or when there is an investigation going on. That is similar to using gemstones to pelt birds for a meal.

CONNECT TO THEIR WORLD

The CRM strategies will be effective and relevant to your customers if you are connected to their world. In considering this, be aware of the need to practice the Tool box approach mentioned in this book. Each line of business will always have unique requirements and appropriate customisation becomes key, in applying CRM principles.

Customer Visits
- Get out of your own world and away from that desk, visit their farm, mine or factory. Have first-hand appreciation of their business, be aware of what affects them and from where they derive their income.
- Where possible, knowing their family and their social interests will always guide you in personalising the responses as well as the respect and attention they might expect you to attach to the experiences you offer them. When things go wrong, like they sometimes do, your strength in this area can become a very big resource to restore good relations with your customers.

Share the Moments
- Join the queue, consume the products and services they also consume. Appreciate how your service makes them feel.

5-Star Customer Service

- Celebrate the important days in their business or lives; share their loss and be a source of comfort – send them a card or some flowers, visit them.
- Invite them to share in your special events like anniversaries, focus groups, golf days and other platforms you use to interact with your external stakeholders.

Virtual Meeting Places (VMPs)

- There are different places where people meet and socialise. The world now has new and growing Virtual Meeting Places (VMPs), via internet and mobile phone technologies. Examples of VMPs include LinkedIn, Twitter, Facebook, Whatsapp, Skype, Google+, Viber and other social media, information sharing and communication channels.
- Use these, not primarily to sell to them, but to interact, socialise, strengthen relations, celebrate your mutual successes, get feedback in an informal set-up, reward and commending them for their custom.
- The biggest benefits to you, include easier access to the customers and growing your understanding of their current and future needs and expectations, so you can offer relevant and personalised experiences best suited to please them.

- If you are going to derive any benefit from your effort, your presence on VMPs must have clearly defined goals.

FEEDBACK SYSTEMS

You can only please your customers when you do exactly what they expect or what they have requested. This can only be possible if you listen to them, and that means giving them the opportunities and platforms to give you their views.

Induction Approach
- Supplying and consuming customers' induction or open-day must be designed to ensure maximum value-addition.
- Zappos pay new employees (internal customers) to leave the company during their period of induction, if the employees see themselves not fitting in with the culture.
- **Is your induction seriously choreographed or it's just a formality?**

Meetings & Other Platforms
- As minimum standards, sections within the organisation must meet on a weekly basis, departments on a monthly basis and interdepartmental service level meetings conducted at least quarterly to discuss performance and service issues.

- Scheduled weekly management meetings are necessary to ensure service and performance is planned and tracked on a regular basis.
- Hold very short daily morning briefs to review the previous day and highlight key issues for the day.
- Customer-interaction functions – luncheons, golf days and year-end cocktails must be used to strengthen customer relationships.
- Interact with customers using a combination of channels including magazines, newsletters, websites – the Culture Book at Zappos.com addressing the meaning of the organisation's attitude to each person and each individual's understanding shared with everyone else.
- Record and share the stories that inspire and re-inforce excellence in service practices. Invest in a library with an accessible collection of literature, books and CDs, which help to empower the desired culture.
- Wall hangings and posters can be used as constant reminders of your commitment.

Customer Loyalty Programs (CLPs)

- **Strategic Partnerships** – over a period of time, you must build useful strategic partnerships that can support your CLPs. An example is the partnership between OK Zimbabwe Ltd and its supplying customers to make the annual *"OK Grand Challenge Promotion"* a success.

- **Personalised Rewards** – the printing of customers' names on corporate gifts, like diaries and pens, is an example of personalised rewards. This also applies to specific gifts for the special anniversaries or birthdays.

- **Personalised Relationships** – your visits, cards, flowers and fruit baskets for anniversaries or when they are hospitalised will enhance relationships at a more personalised level.

- **Incentivised Rewards** – point cards issued by hotels, flying miles given by airline companies, discounts applicable if you pay use a card with loyalty benefits or every fifth trip offered free by some luxury coaches, are all rewards meant to encourage more frequent usage of underlying products or services and create customer loyalty.

LEARNING QUESTIONS

1. How are you promoting Customer Loyalty? What else can you start doing?

2. If you have a CLP, what lessons have you drawn, how effective have your programs been?

LEARNING STORY

The founder and Group CEO of Nyaradzo Funeral Assurance Company, Philip Mataranyika, worked for a leading Financial services company during the same period I was with the same organisation. He was in the Individual Life business and I was in the Employee Benefits division. I remember my manager giving a free presentation on Mr Mataranyika's 5-Star brand, whenever he drove past.

My manager would always tell stories about how this 5-Star performer was able to buy himself the same Mercedes Benz edition as the company's CEO. The story was that his income was largely commission-based, making him the best business development consultant of his era, and some phenomenal dollar figures would be quoted! This self-assigned, Philip Mataranyika business biographer, would explain how he was targeting students in particular professions by selling the benefits of his products, he would continue building these relationships with them until they graduated and flourished in their careers.

This CRM model would then form a quality pipeline over a period of time, helping in sustaining the growth of his portfolio and the flow of income. Philip Mataranyika was a 5-Star CRM and Sales performer, winning the company Chairman's Top Financial Advisor award, for five consecutive years, from 1996 until he left to start Nyaradzo in 2001.

It is therefore, not surprising to see this personal effectiveness story reflect through the phenomenal growth of Nyaradzo, from a small new entrant, translating into Zimbabwe's largest, and still growing, Funeral assurance player.

By branding themselves *"Sahwira Mukuru"* or *"Best Friend"* and giving each bereaved family a memorial tree, Nyaradzo has shown innovation in their CRM strategy, ensuring something remains a reminder of the loved one who passed on as well as an example of practical compassion from a *"Best Friend"* during times of need.

Integrated Technology Interfaces (ITIs)

The current and future levels of technological interface means information about anything and anyone can be available in any part of the world at the press of a button.

My stints in accounting and IT technical training exposed me to the way technology can be employed to make computer systems interface or *'talk'* to each other. The systems become integrated when they are brought together, and more so, opened up to become accessible to multiple users.

Types of CRM Systems

There are various types of systems to suit different organisations and their unique requirements. Systems cab be grouped as follows:

1. Internally installed but externally hosted system.
2. Stand-alone CRM application, interfaced with other business management systems.
3. CRM application integrated into the core Business Management System.

Importance of CRM Systems

1. Enables the organisation to provide a real-time picture and online information on each customer by connecting the various sources within and outside the organisation.
2. Makes it possible for each employee to access information appropriate to their level of authority and their area of responsibility.
3. Empowers employees with the tools to make quick informed decisions and to customise/personalise the service experience for each customer.
4. Redirecting of more time to productive efforts, as a CRM system helps minimise administrative challenges and bureaucratic processes.

Choosing a CRM System

Below, are some tips to help you choose the best CRM technology for your unique requirements:-

1. Define your business needs, guided by the needs of your customers and stakeholders.
2. Lay-out the benefits and outcomes you expect to get from the CRM system.
3. Determine the quality of reports and usefulness of statistics, as determined by your requirements.

4. Make sure it will be easy to create an interface with other business management and operations systems.
5. Be satisfied that it will be easy to customise system parameters to suit your dynamic business needs. What is the quality and efficiency level of the supplier's customer support service?
6. On your part, ensure proper orientation of staff, data integrity at both, input and processing stages.

LEARNING QUESTIONS

1. Do you have a Business Management System in place? How much automated or computerised is it? Does it include CRM functions?
2. How well integrated or interfaced is your BMS? Can it 'talk' to other relevant systems and is it accessible to all key users within or outside your organisation?
3. How much information and service can you offer customers at their convenience, on the backbone of your ICT systems?

Chapter 14

CREATING A 5-STAR CUSTOMER SERVICE CULTURE

"Whatever your hands find to do, do it with all your might; for there is no work or device or knowledge or wisdom in the grave where you are going"
–THE HOLY BIBLE

Service delivery/performance alone is not enough – demonstrate how hospitable you are and build long-lasting relationships.

"You can't just ask customers what they want and then try to give that to them. By the time you get it built, they'll want something new"
- STEVE JOBS

"There is a 60%-70% probability of selling to an existing customer than to a new prospect."
- MARKETING METRICS

5-STAR CUSTOMER SERVICE CULTURE

"...culture became our number one priority, even more important than customer service. We thought that if we got the culture right, then building our brand to be about the very best customer service would happen naturally on its own. To keep our culture strong, we wanted to make sure we only hired people who we would also enjoy hanging out with outside the office...Every year, a new edition of the Zappos Culture Book is produced, which we give out to prospective employees, vendors, and even customers."
-TONY HSIEH | DELIVERING HAPPINESS

The Goal

"Ideally we want all 10 core values to be reflected in everything we do, including how we interact with each other, how we interact with our customers, and how we interact with our vendors and business partners...it will be quite some time before our 10 core values are truly reflected in how we think, how we act and how we communicate. As we grow, our processes and strategies may change, but we want our values to always remain the same. Our core values should always be the framework from which we make all our decisions."
-TONY HSIEH | CEO, ZAPPOS.COM

WHAT THE BEST IN THE WORLD ARE DOING

Zappos.com Core Values
(An example of Core Values capable of carrying and sustaining a Culture of Service Excellence)

1. Deliver WOW Through Service.
2. Embrace and Drive Change.
3. Create Fun and A Little Weirdness.
4. Be Adventurous, Creative, and Open-Minded.
5. Pursue Growth and Learning.
6. Build Open and Honest Relationships With Communication.
7. Build a Positive Team and Family Spirit.
8. Do More With Less.
9. Be Passionate and Determined.
10. Be Humble.

THE COCA COLA WINNING CULTURE
(What drives the winning culture of the world's best-selling non-essential product?)[7]

Our Winning Culture

Our Winning Culture defines the attitudes and behaviors that will be required of us to make our 2020 Vision a reality.

Live Our Values

Our values serve as a compass for our actions and describe how we behave in the world.

- **Leadership**: The courage to shape a better future.
- **Collaboration**: Leverage collective genius.
- **Integrity**: Be real.
- **Accountability**: If it is to be, it's up to me.
- **Passion**: Committed in heart and mind.
- **Diversity**: As inclusive as our brands.
- **Quality**: What we do, we do well.

Focus on the Market

- Focus on needs of our consumers, customers and franchise partners.
- Get out into the market and listen, observe and learn.
- Possess a world view.
- Focus on execution in the marketplace every day.
- Be insatiably curious.

Work Smart

- Act with urgency.
- Remain responsive to change.
- Have the courage to change course when needed.
- Remain constructively discontent.
- Work efficiently.

Act Like Owners

1. Be accountable for our actions and inactions.
2. Steward system assets and focus on building value.
3. Reward our people for taking risks and finding better ways to solve problems.
4. Learn from our outcomes -- what worked and what didn't.

Be the Brand

- Inspire creativity, passion, optimism and fun.

5-STAR CUSTOMER SERVICE GOAL
To create loyal customers for life

"If you would ask me what my goal in writing this book is, this would be my short answer – To challenge you to consider different ways and principles which help you create loyal customers for life. Because lifetime loyal customers are the fuel that has sustained the world's multi-generation brands since time immemorial."
ARCHIBALD MARWIZI

INITIATIVES TO IMPROVE SERVICE

1. **Reflecting on the Concepts, Examples and Case Studies** covered in this book. What customer service initiatives can you begin to implement within your organisation:

    a. At a Personal Level
    b. At a Departmental Level
    c. At a Group Level

2. **Promoting a 5-Star Customer Service Culture**
 a) Which internal initiatives, competitions and awards, can you introduce to promote improved customer service?
 b) How can you start developing Customer Loyalty Programs to strengthen your relationship with external customers?
 c) Come up with an effective program to frequently manage customer feedback and improve quality of service through the effective use of Surveys, Suggestion boxes, email, website and other VMP feedback mechanisms.
 d) Draft and implement a policy and processes that ensure efficient and effective After-sales service.
 e) Craft or refine your Customer Service Charter in consultation with key stakeholders, and have an official launch. Ensure delivery and evaluation processes are effected.
 f) Come up with unique services or experiences for your department or organisation to enhance the quality of memorable customer experiences you deliver. Consider the example of the RTG greeting and the Boma party.

5-Star Customer Service

g) Schedule and conduct customer visits for your portfolio, where possible, leave "Thank you" cards just to appreciate their custom. You can alternatively send emails or make phone calls.

h) Create and conduct customer-focus group sessions or open day sessions for your department. Use their input and feedback to improve your products and services to become more customised to customers' needs.

i) Consult with your IT partners and embark on a project to create personalised tech-platforms to improve virtual interaction with customers as well as extend added convenience, including access to information like statements, payment options and online services.

j) Define the Service Culture you envision your customers getting exposed to. Look for development material, including books and begin building your departmental or group library. Encourage presentation of book summaries during team meetings and link this element to each individual's personal development goals.

k) Identify, train and assign capable individuals to become 5-Star Customer Service Champions. Give them badges, special neck ties or any emblem that can make it easy to notice them as well as making the whole process an inspiring adventure.

l) Create a book or blog site which can be updated with stories, from both employees and customers, on the great customer service experiences shared over a period of time. If resources permit, get it printed and distributed to customers and staff to continue inspiring a culture of 5-Star Customer Service.

m) Train new employees on the 5-Star Customer Service and CRM principles and run refresher training for existing employees. This will ensure a consistent generation and flow of fresh ideas within the organisation.

n) Your sense of imagination and creative abilities do not have to be limited by the above - be creative and add your own ideas to what you have found in this book!

WHAT THE BEST IN THE WORLD ARE DOING

♦ The General Electric (GE) Beliefs

The Best are guided by Inspiring Beliefs:

1. Customers determine success.
2. Stay lean to go fast.
3. Learn and adapt to win.
4. Empower and inspire each other.
5. Deliver results in an uncertain world.

♦ The Google Truths

From *"Ten things we know to be true"* as part of the Google values and Charter, I take the first one. Simple and straight to the point.

1. ***"Focus on the user (customer) and all else will follow."***

- **Bring your team together, physically or virtually.**

- **Anticipate Future Customer Needs.**

- **Share the special Stories about your Customers' Experiences.**

LEARNING QUESTIONS

1. What story are you creating and telling? How inspiring is your Customer Service Culture?

2. How can you use technology, to create one-stop-shop platforms or service areas for your customers?

3. Write a Case Study or Case Studies based on the stories of great service and customer experiences generated within your organisation.

5-Star Customer Service

THE 10 COMMANDMENTS OF 5-STAR CUSTOMER SERVICE

The 10 Commandments of 5-Star Customer Service below, summarise the principles covered in this book:

1. Have a thorough understanding of the needs and expectations of your customers.

2. Develop and refine the customer service skills and knowledge within your organization.

3. Invest in providing consistent memorable experiences.

4. Excel in intrapersonal and interpersonal communication skills.

5. Continuously develop the personal brands of your staff and ensure they adopt a positive attitude at all times.

6. Craft and improve policies, systems, processes and standards, to systematize the provision of excellent service.

7. Create and manage internal and external relationships to create loyalty and value-added interactions – extend the same to personal relationships.

8. Ensure senior management commitment and inspire every team member to focus on a shared vision, with passion.

9. Create a culture of performance excellence, by practicing customer-focused values in fulfilment of your mission and strategic objectives.

10. Enjoy serving customers from the heart, every day - and you will excel.

I dream of a world with 5-Star Customer Service provided in government ministries, department and offices, in prisons and police stations. It has already begun, who knows, next it will be OF HOMES AND MAIDS...dream on!

Other Books by the Same Author

Access the following books by the same author:
1. Making Success Deliberate –
   a. How To Develop & Sustain A Personal Effectiveness and Leadership Excellence Brand.
   b. Workplace Effectiveness
   c. The 3 Keys to Growth, Profits and Sustained Success.
2. Making Success Deliberate – The Divine Connection Series.
   a. Pursuing God's Perfect Will For Your Life
   b. Becoming Active Covenant Partners With God
   c. Leading From The Heart of God
   d. Stretching Your Mind to See The Invisible & Do The Impossible
   e. Wisdom – The Master Craftsman of Success
3. Difficult but Possible: Overcoming Life's Relentless Challenges (The Story of my Life).
4. Stop. Think. Use your Brain.
5. I Want To Change! – How To Sustain a Positive Change In Habits, Behaviour, Feelings & Attitude.

Visit:
www.fivestar.co.zw
www.archiemarwizi.com

Your Comments Are Welcome:
archie@fivestar.co.zw
gudmsd@gmail.com

Let's Connect Where The World Is Gathering:
Facebook: www.facebook.com/archibald.marwizi
LinkedIn: Archibald Marwizi
Google+: Archie Marwizi
Twitter: @archiemarwizi
Skype: archie.marwizi

About The Author

"HI!"

"My name is Archie from 5-Star Services wishing you all the best in your personal and corporate endeavors, and above all, a successful journey towards a 5-Star Service Culture. For all your talent and organisational development needs, we are available as your partners in attaining your corporate goals. We look forward to seeing you in our 5-Star Workshops and thank you for trusting us with your personal development."

Archibald T. Marwizi

Archie is an Author, Corporate Trainer and Speaker. He is the Managing Director of Gudbank and Founder of 5-Star Training Workshops. His experience in leadership, management, human resources development, project management, retail banking and consulting spans over two decades. Archie has contributed his expertise in private and public companies across the economic sectors, parastatals and government departments, and has been excited by the difference he is making through donor-funded programs aimed to assist local authorities improve service delivery in Africa.

He is accredited to run Zimhost and Afrihost training workshops and has been involved in the launching of Ugahost (Uganda), Zamhost (Zambia) and holds the franchise for Naijahost (Nigeria).

REFERENCE NOTES/INDEX

1. 5-Star Customer Service Framework Diagram - Diagram Design adapted from Equitas - International Centre for Human Rights Education, Training of Trainers: Designing & Delivering Effective Human Rights Education – 2007 Training Manual.

2. The Power of a Smile – re-adapted from How To Win Friends and Influence People – Dale Carnegie.

3. (a) The story of Sainsbury's Tiger Bread - *Sainsbury Tiger bread* (Story adapted from https://threescore.files.wordpress.com/2011/06/connelly.jpg and http://www.j-sainsbury.co.uk/media/latest-stories/2012/20120131-why-were-renaming-tiger-bread-to-giraffe-bread/).

4. (a) The ExtraCity Luxury stories and examples as recorded from interactions with the company and adapted with permission from Dave & Fari Masimira.

    (b) 2015 "Letters to the Editor" section of The Chronicle, Zimbabwe Newspapers. Letter from Sikoliwe Scotch Nyathi, Nkandebwe Hills, Hwange - titled "Hats off to ExtraCity bus service management"

5. Definition of Service - Microsoft® Encarta® 2009. © 1993-2008 Microsoft Corporation. All rights reserved.

6. The Story of Zappos.com and Tony Hsieh quotations from the book, *"Delivering Happiness - A Path to Profits, Passion and Purpose"* adapted with permission from the "Delivering Happiness Team."

7. The Coca Cola examples and "The Winning Culture" from http://www.coca-colacompany.com/our-company/diversity/workplace-culture.

8. The Attributes of Emotional Intelligence - *Adapted from "Primal Leadership – Realising the Power of Emotional Intelligence" by Daniel Goleman with Richard Boyatzis and Annie McKee.*

5-Star Customer Service

9. (a) The ISO 9000 Quality Management Standards family, lessons from the International Organisation for Standardisation (ISO), http://www.iso.org accessed 28/08/2015.

   (b) Summary of what ISO 9001:2015 covers - http://asq.org/learn-about-quality/iso-9000/overview/overview.html, accesses 19/09/2015.

10. Malcolm Baldrige Criteria for Performance Excellence - The 7 Categories, adapted from Baldrige National Quality Program – www.quality.nist.gov

11. Bulawayo City Council Learning Story - "Bowser Restores Water, Sanitation And Hygiene Services In Bulawayo" - Report From Australian Agency For International Development (Australian AID, http://reliefweb.int/organisation/ausaid) - Published On 18 Apr 2013.

12. Citizen Charters

    a) Definition of a Citizen or Customer Service Charter – (i) adapted and paraphrased from Microsoft® Encarta® 2009. © 1993-2008 Microsoft Corporation. All rights reserved.
    (ii) Citizen Charter Handbook, Centre For Good Governance, Government of India.

    b) Basic Concept, Origin and Principles of Citizen Charters –

    i. The Citizen's Charter: Raising the Standard, presented to Parliament by the Prime Minister by Command of Her Majesty, July 1991, London, England.

    ii. The Citizen's Charter: First Report: 1992, presented to Parliament by the Prime Minister and the Chancellor of the Duchy of Lancaster by Command of Her Majesty, November 1992, London, England.

    iii. The Citizen Charter Handbook - Centre for Good Governance, Government of India.

13. Analytical CRM and Behavioural CRM (quotations in italics) – as distinguished and defined in the Paper titled,

"Choice Models and Customer Relationship Management" by WAGNER KAMAKURA et al. – (Marketing Letters 16:3/4, 279–291, 2005 c 2005 Springer Science + Business Media, Inc. Manufactured in the Netherlands.)

14. General Electric Beliefs – accessed from, www.ge.com on 21/03/2015.

15. The Google Truths – accessed from, https://www.google.com on 28/03/2015.

16. Statistics adapted from various sources and surveys, including:

    a) CRM Magazine – accessed from, http://www.destinationcrm.com/Articles/ReadArticle.aspx?ArticleID=90678 on 20/03/2015.
    b) Touch Agency – accessed from, http://www.helpscout.net/blog/?utm_source=75stats-ebook&utm_medium=download&utm_campaign=75stats-ebook on 22/03/2015
    c) The Social Customer Engagement Index –
    d) IBM Digital Customer Experience Report – accessed from, http://www.slideshare.net/IBMDigitalExperience/teafleafinfographicr6-140827100411phpapp02 on 20/03/2015.
    e) Benchmark Portal – accessed from, http://www.helpscout.net/blog/?utm_source=75stats-ebook&utm_medium=download&utm_campaign=75stats-ebook on 22/03/2015.
    f) Marketing Metrics – accessed from, http://www.helpscout.net/blog/?utm_source=75stats-ebook&utm_medium=download&utm_campaign=75stats-ebook on 22/03/2015.
    g) Forrester Research INC. – accessed from, http://www.aspect.com/Documents/Papers/Aspect-NGCC-Forrester-WP.pdf on 20/03/2015.
    h) State of Multichannel Customer Service Survey – accessed from, http://ww2.parature.com/lp/report-2014-state-multichannel-cs-survey-comm.html on 20/03/2015.
    i) Contact Point Client Research

j) Ernst & Young – Customer Centricity Paper, The journey toward greater customer centricity, accessed from on 24/03/2015.
k) Accent Marketing – accessed from, http://misgl.com/blog, on 24/03/2015.
l) Accenture – accessed from, http://www.accenture.com/SiteCollectionDocuments/PDF/Accenture-Maximizing-Customer-Retention.pdf on 20/03/2015.
m) Bain & Company – accessed from, http://www.bain.com/publications/business-insights/loyalty.aspx, on 20/03/2015.
n) McKinsey – accessed from, http://returnonbehavior.com/2010/10/50-facts-about-customer-experience-for-2011/ on 20/03/2015.
o) NewVoiceMedia – accessed from, http://www.smartcustomerservice.com/Articles/News-Briefs/Research-U.S.-Businesses-Lose-$41-Billion-Annually-Due-to-Poor-Customer-Service-93869.aspx on 20/03/2015.
p) Harris Interactive/Right Now – accessed from, http://www.slideshare.net/RightNow/2011-customer-experience-impact-report, on 20/03/2015.
q) Ruby Newell-Legner – accessed from, http://www.rubyspeaks.com/bio.asp on 20/03/2015.
r) INFINIT Contact – accessed from, http://www.infinitcontact.com/blog, on 20/03/2015.
s) Merlin – accessed from, http://misgl.com/blog, on 24/03/2015.
t) Lee Resources – accessed from, http://www.helpscout.net/blog/?utm_source=75stats-ebook&utm_medium=download&utm_campaign=75stats-ebook on 22/03/2015.
u) American Express Survey – accessed from, http://about.americanexpress.com/news/docs/2012x/axp_2012gcsb_us.pdf on 20/03/2015.
v) Customer 2020 Report – accessed from, http://www.walkerinfo.com/customers2020/ on 20/03/2015.
w) Emmet & Mark Murphy – From the book, *"Leading on the Edge of Chaos."* http://www.amazon.com/Leading-Edge-Chaos-Critical-Elements/dp/0735203121

x) Genesys Global Survey - accessed from, http://www.help-scout.net/blog/?utm_source=75stats-ebook&utm_medium=download&utm_campaign=75stats-ebook on 22/03/2015.

-THE END-

www.ingramcontent.com/pod-product-compliance
Lightning Source LLC
Chambersburg PA
CBHW070851180526
45168CB00005B/1775